IN THE COMPANY OF GIANTS

IN THE COMPANY OF GIANTS

CANDID CONVERSATIONS WITH THE VISIONARIES OF THE DIGITAL WORLD

RAMA D. JAGER

RAFAEL ORTIZ

McGraw-Hill
New York   San Francisco   Washington, D.C.   Auckland   Bogotá
Caracas   Lisbon   London   Madrid   Mexico City   Milan
Montreal   New Delhi   San Juan   Singapore
Sydney   Tokyo   Toronto

Library of Congress Cataloging-in-Publication Data

Jager, Rama Dev.
    In the company of giants : candid conversations with the
visionaries of the digital world / Rama Dev Jager, Rafael Ortiz.
        p.   cm.
    ISBN 0-07-032934-6
    1. Computer industry—United States—Management—Case studies.
2. Computer software industry—United States—Management—Case
studies.   3. Entrepreneurship—United States—Case studies.
4. Success in business—United States—Case studies.   5. Chief
executive officers—United States—Interviews.   I. Ortiz, Rafael
(Rafael G.)   II. Title
HD9696.C63U51865   1997
004′.068′4—dc21   97-1906
                                                                     CIP

McGraw-Hill

A Division of The McGraw-Hill Companies

    2 3 4 5 6 7 8 9 0   DOC/DOC   9 0 2 1 0 9 8 7

ISBN 0-07-032934-6

*The sponsoring editor for this book was Susan Barry, the editing supervisor
was Fred Bernardi, and the production supervisor was Suzanne W. B.
Rapcavage. It was set in Fairfield by Terry Leaden of McGraw-Hill's
Professional Book Group composition unit.*

Printed and bound by R. R. Donnelley & Sons Company.

This publication is designed to provide accurate and authoritative information in regard to the subject matter covered. It is sold with the understanding that the publisher is not engaged in rendering legal, accounting,
or other professional service. If legal advice or other expert assistance is
required, the services of a competent professional person should be
sought.
                —From a declaration of principles jointly adopted by a committee
                    of the American Bar Association and a committee of publishers.

*Trademarks and registered trademarks mentioned in this book are the
copyrighted property of their respective companies.*

*To my mother—who, in spite of all of these giants,
remains the primary source of my inspiration.*
—RDJ

*To my parents, who taught me to read, and to Lisa,
for teaching me what it means to write.*
—RGO

CONTENTS

ACKNOWLEDGMENTS

For innumerable reasons, our sincere appreciation goes to Rama's father, Dr. Rama M. Jager, and to Irv Grousbeck, Andy Grove, and Ed Lazear. Without them, we never would have been able to create *Giants*.

We are grateful to our editor at McGraw-Hill, Susan Barry, who believed in two fresh first-time authors, and to our agent, Sheryl Fullerton, who patiently steered our exuberant, chaotic efforts in the general direction of a book.

Rafael's wife, Lisa, graciously offered advice, support, and much-needed reprimands—"Strunk and White wouldn't like that"—all while keeping her own writing career from being derailed by ours, no small feat.

Rama (Dev) thanks his mother, Dr. Nirmala M. Ray, for her support throughout the entire process—but mostly for her belief in me. Rama also thanks two role models: Dr. Robert Burnett and Dr. Lee Shahinian, Jr., and the rest of the EMCard team, for their patience in dealing with *Giants* while running a startup.

For advice, guidance, and candid feedback we'd like to thank Connie Bagley, David Bradford, Robert Burgelman, Steve Butler, Dennis Coleman, Ann Crichton, Rohit Deshpande, Jim and Marilyn Lattin, George Parker, Steve Piersante, Garth Saloner, and Diane Savage.

In addition, we would like to thank three executives who generously gave us time and guidance during the early phases of the project, but regrettably could not be included in *Giants*: Heidi Roizen (former CEO of T/Maker, current head of Apple Developer Relations), Walter Loewenstern and Ken Oshman (co-founders of ROLM).

Finally, we thank the CEOs who agreed to be a part of *Giants*. Their time is perhaps their most precious resource, and we are grateful for their generosity with it both during our interviews and after, when we needed answers to "just one more question." By sharing their experiences, they have taught us tremendously.

PREFACE

The professor asked, with a wide grin, "So you want to write a book on high-tech CEOs? Well, gentlemen, it's a long shot. A huge long shot. And, besides...no CEO knows why he is successful. It's all just luck."

On a balmy day in mid-spring, we were two Stanford MBA students trying hard to conceal our disappointment. Coming from a well-known strategic management professor, a comment such as this seemed somewhat ridiculous—for if successful management were all luck, then why were we taking his class? Why, for that matter, were we in business school? Surely, successful management was not entirely due to luck—there had to be some successful strategy and ideas at play too.

Louis Pasteur once said that chance favors the prepared mind. If "chance" is a major factor in a company's success, as our professor believed, then we really wanted to know what successful entrepreneurs do to "prepare" their minds.

What are the crucial skills needed to run a successful company? To hire great people? To ship a great product? What skills should a potential manager try to develop? Why was one manager successful where another wasn't? Answers to these questions, in the words of the very people who have started succcessful technology companies, comprise this book.

WHO WE CHOSE TO SPEAK WITH AND WHY WE CHOSE THEM

Bill Gates. Andy Grove. Bill Hewlett. Steve Jobs. Why them? Why not others?

Hundreds of entrepreneurs have had great ideas and have started great companies. What differentiates the vast majority of entrepreneurs profiled in this book is that they not only have started their respective companies, but also have had an active role in the company's growth. These entrepreneurs weren't booted out of the company after starting it—they *weren't* people who had one great original idea, implemented it, and left because they weren't good managers. Instead, they had a great idea, managed the team that implemented the idea, and then had *another* great idea and managed the team that implemented *that* idea. They transformed the company from a "one-great-product" company to a "two-or-more-great-products" company; they made the company *grow*—they not only planted the seed, they watered the plant.

We chose to focus on the computer industry for two reasons. First and foremost, computers are dynamically changing the way people exist. They are causing *generational change*. Compared to our parents—who use computers for word processing or technical applications at best—many of us use the power of computers for surfing the internet, communicating with friends and colleagues, and balancing a checkbook.

Second, going to Stanford's business school put us in the heart of Silicon Valley. Steve Jobs candidly told us one night, "Well, if you're at heaven's gate, you might as well walk inside and take a peek."

WHAT OUR BOOK ATTEMPTS TO DO

Reading this book is not an instant path to guaranteed wealth. Notice that this book is *not* entitled *How to Start a Billion-Dollar Computer Company*, or *How to Get Rich Quick Off Chips*. Such titles do not genuinely help us convey the messages of this book.

What we *do* want to convey are stories of some of the

greatest entrepreneurs in history. Their companies directly influence the way we live, what we do, and even what we can't do. Instead of focusing on these companies, *In the Company of Giants* focuses on leaders—we attempted to discern *who* the person was behind the company, what his or her style of management was, and whether this conflicted with, or conformed to, conventional startup wisdom. Looking at the people behind these companies is one small way of interpreting the revolutionary technological change that the world is experiencing today.

Rama D. Jager
Rafael Ortiz

IN THE COMPANY OF GIANTS

FROM SAND TO GOLD

A BRIEF AND RELEVANT HISTORY OF THE HIGH-TECH INDUSTRY

On January 22, 1984, 100 million people were watching the Los Angeles Raiders as they crushed the Washington Redskins 38-9 in Super Bowl XXVIII. The halftime show, a made-for-TV extravaganza, proved but a sidelight to the production value of the television advertisements that elbowed their way into viewers' living rooms.

One such commercial, never aired again, stood above the rest and branded the nation's collective consciousness.

In it, gray brainwashed automatons marched toward a gigantic screen of sinister Big Brother (a thinly veiled IBM) rhapsodizing about "everybody using one standard." Out of the shadows, a lone woman, clearly not indoctrinated like those around her, charges and hurls a sledgehammer at his projected image. The result: a shattered false oracle and newfound freedom for the oppressed masses. The somewhat surreal Orwellian ad ends with a voice proclaiming, "On January 24th, Apple Computer will introduce Macintosh. And you'll see why 1984 won't be like '1984.'"

Literally a smashing success, this ad promoted the alternative to an IBM-centric vision of computing and launched

Apple Computer's next generation of personal computing, the Apple Macintosh.

Part of that commercial's and eventually, the Macintosh's, success was because of Apple's chairman, Steve Jobs. That year, Jobs formally unveiled the Macintosh at the company's annual shareholder meeting in Cupertino, California. With showman's style, he unveiled the Macintosh computer—capable of accepting user commands using a graphical, desktop interface and manipulated by the user with menu-based commands. No more obscure keyboard commands. No more rat's nest of wires and cables. It was a hit.

As one attendee of that emotive shareholder's meeting told us, "You can't begin to understand the emotional intensity in the auditorium that day. Remember that the place was crowded with hundreds of disgruntled Apple employees still reeling from the failure of the Lisa [Apple's first attempt at graphics-based computing] and dozens of cynical analysts from New York who'd seen and heard it all. I can tell you this: at the end of the meeting, everybody was on their feet wildly cheering. There wasn't a dry eye in the house."

Jobs and others like him in this book have created companies that have skyrocketed to glory. What are their secrets? Is it just luck? Though fortune undeniably plays a role in all ventures, the ability to start and grow one or more companies in the tumultuous, rollicking computer industry takes some talent. Indeed, considering that as many as 90 percent of new firms fail within five years, it's more appropriate to recognize that the Giants profiled in this book were both beneficiaries and creators of luck. Collectively, their companies command almost $100 billion in yearly revenues.

As the industrial age had its magnates, the information age boasts its own pantheon of self-made barons. This chapter provides a brief history of the contemporary American computer industry and the businesspeople who shaped it. By orienting you, the reader, with the story behind the computers we work and play with, we hope to contextualize this industry's amazing growth and the people who led it.

By the mid-1970s, California's Santa Clara orchards gave

way to an onslaught of commercial construction. New companies and newly minted millionaires crowded Silicon Valley and the Route 128 area outside of Boston. It was the dawn of a new era in American capitalism, a new gold rush.

But this was a gold rush of a different sort: Instead of racing to extract precious metals from the ground, young opportunists converted sand's base substance, silicon, into microchip components, pound-for-pound worth more than gold. Others with Midas-like insight crafted lengthy, cryptic messages using these very microchips, to automate heretofore time-consuming, manual administrative work.

It is difficult to meaningfully convey the extent to which computers have evolved and shaped our daily march through life. Intel co-founder Gordon Moore put it in perspective by describing the phenomenon commonly known as "Moore's Law." This principle states that the number of transistors—and therefore the computing power—per microprocessor will double every 18 months.

To illustrate this point, consider that the raw computational power of IBM's powerful, million-dollar mainframes in the '70s today fits into the diminutive package of a handheld calculator. It is this incredible development that has fueled the unprecedented change in business processes the world-over. Moore's Law is in full effect.

Ironically, many of the stories of successful entrepreneurs were not born from master plans for world domination but of sheer frustration with the ineptitude, politics and mediocrity of the companies they abandoned.

Case in point: Thomas Watson, Sr., IBM's spiritual father, was fired earlier in his career by his previous firm's jealous and arbitrary executive. Undaunted, he founded a promising card tabulating company and in his disciplined, autocratic manner, led the company to incredible heights. His company's early domination of the computer industry created tremendous wealth for IBM shareholders. At a 1954 shareholder meeting, Watson remarked:

A purchase of 100 shares in 1914 would have cost

$2,750...This would now amount to 3,114 shares, with a market value of $1,029,177, which with cash dividends of $117,356 paid during this period, totals $1,206,533...

In perfect irony, IBM's success generated its competition: a young MIT graduate student working on a joint computer development project with IBM for the Department of Defense. His frustration with IBM's stuffy hierarchy and approach to computing drove him to realize his own vision of computing—he fundamentally believed that individuals wanted their own access to the computer, with a keyboard and monitor, rather than ceding control to computer systems operators. This young man, Ken Olsen, created the basis for the next generation in computing, minicomputers. Named that because of their relatively small physical size and ability to work without special air conditioning, minicomputers also happened to be very low cost—DEC's sub-$100,000 system price was a relative bargain compared with IBM's million-dollar hardware. Digital's runaway success earned Olsen, his venture capitalists, and lucky investors millions.

Digital's ascent inspired dozens of imitators and competitors and, only 22 years after the company's founding, sparked the imagination of a 12-year-old boy at Seattle's Lakeside School—Bill Gates. His introduction to computing: Digital's PDP-8 computer.

Despite the apparently boundless opportunity that awaited promising computer industry startups, roadkill littered the road to dominance in the nascent industry. William Shockley, the Nobel Prize-winning co-inventor of the transistor (a miniaturized vacuum tube set in a single solid piece of germanium—later silicon) was among the most notable business failures.

Previously, all computers used vacuum tube technology as processors of information. One of the first computers ever developed, ENIAC, was a 30 ton, 1,500 square foot, unreliable monstrosity. With Shockley Semiconductor's (as the firm was called) technology, more compact and powerful computers could be built using thousands and thousands of microscopic circuits.

Shockley's skills as a physicist didn't necessarily translate into management talent, however. After only a couple of years in business, his firm suffered defections from bright young engineers. Among the defectors were Robert Noyce and Gordon Moore, who with a handful of other engineers founded Fairchild Semiconductor.

Fairchild's role as the standard-bearer of semiconductor technology paradoxically proved to be its own undoing. Dozens of other starry-eyed developers left to start their own companies. Again Noyce and Moore departed, and with a young Hungarian-born physicist named Andy Grove in tow, created Intel (INTegrated ELectronics). Many Silicon Valley startups of that era trace their lineage back to Fairchild.

Intel's first products were advanced memory chips. Later, it devised a way to put all of the circuits that worked as the main processors for a computer onto a single chip. The company was slow to recognize the importance of its achievement, but it eventually focused its business solely on this technology and grew to amass industry dominance by selling its successive generations of "microprocessors" to the world's largest personal computer manufacturers.

Unnoticed by most, the January 1975 issue of *Popular Electronics* heralded the arrival of the next, albeit primitive, generation of computing: a computer kit priced affordably enough for hobbyists to assemble their very own machine and use it to perform modest calculations. The cowboy entrepreneur behind this computer, the Altair, was Ed Roberts. His company, MITS, cleverly leveraged Intel's microprocessor developments by incorporating the Intel 8080 as the brains for its low-cost machine.

To all outward appearances, the little Altair was a black box. Adorned only with flashing red lights to inform the user that it was working on something and lacking a keyboard and monitor, Altair riveted imaginative young minds on the east and west coasts to the potential of personal computing. It was not long after the machine's launch that college undergrad Bill Gates and his partner, Paul Allen, were furiously writing code that would serve as Altair's base operating system, thereby giving users the ability to perform more useful functions with the machine than just flipping toggle switches that made lights blink on and off.

Meanwhile, in the suburbs of the San Francisco Bay Area, young engineers, hackers and assorted minstrels circulated in a subculture of computer tinkering, assembly and idea-sharing. The Homebrew Computer Club was among the most recognized organizations in this milieu. It was there that several enthusiasts studied the Altair and Gates' software, and in fits of technical one-upmanship, developed their own computers. Dozens and dozens of machines were created—some with their own software, others pirated from Gates' work. Few among them viewed these developments as money-making opportunities.

In the early 1970s, Xerox was the paragon of corporate success. Company management rightly concluded that industry leadership would require technical superiority and development leadership. The company set out to create the world's leading corporate research center in the backyard of Stanford University. Its Palo Alto Research Center was known and venerated by all associated with it as Xerox PARC.

Despite PARC's preeminence as a center of leading-edge work in computing, it proved to be the antithesis of entrepreneurial activity as innovation after innovation walked out of PARC's doors to be capitalized on by others. PARC's leadership in graphically-based computer operating systems directly influenced Apple's development of the Macintosh and Microsoft's development of the Windows operating system—both considered among the most influential and lucrative technologies to emerge from the modern computing era.

So, what's in store for the future? The 90s have brought promise of a new era in computing. Simply put, the new paradigm for entrepreneurs to grapple with is the notion that computers connected to others—communicating and sharing information amongst them—increases their value tremendously to users. Steve Case, founder of America Online, saw this in 1985 when he created a proprietary service designed to allow users with modem-equipped computers to communicate with others in a private community setting or to retrieve information from the equivalent of town hall bulletin boards. Case's venture, America Online, grew several years before the rapid popularization of the internet took place. Originally a network of networks, the internet was designed by the military to allow researchers to communicate with other researchers. As the Net's commercialization continued, companies recognized the value of low cost communication by computers over great distances. America Online and now hundreds of others aim to cash in on what promises to be a whole new industry.

As startup ventures sprout like mushrooms in venture capital-backed fecundity, it remains to be seen whether the advent of the internet strengthens the Giants' hold over computing or undermines it to create an entirely new generation of successful entrepreneurs and leaders. Regardless, we think you'll find these candid conversations with some of America's greatest entrepreneurs as informative and entertaining as we did.

1

STEVE JOBS

Apple Computer,
NeXT Software, and Pixar

ONLY THE BEST—PEOPLE, PRODUCT, PURPOSE

The story of Steve Jobs is the story of a young college drop-out who sojourned to India in search of purity and enlightenment, returned to the U.S., and founded Apple Computer. Was dabbling with Hinduism the key to success for a 20-year-old with little money and a modest technical background?

Perhaps. High school buddy Steve Wozniak—by all accounts a brilliant tinkerer and engineer—and Jobs collaborated on several "projects" during their adolescence, including hacking into phone company networks and making video games. Yet, over time, their individual responsibilities remained well-defined: Wozniak mainly designed and built the product, and Jobs scrambled to find customers, coworkers, and components. Eventually the projects became of value to others and Jobs persuaded Wozniak in 1976 to devote his energy to a partnership—Apple Computer.

Many would-be entrepreneurs, lacking money or strong

business experience, become stymied by the challenges of obtaining financing and recruiting people to join in working for what is essentially an idea. Yet Jobs doggedly cajoled suppliers and retail outlets to provide Apple with low pricing and extended credit. His apathy for maintaining his outward appearance—he often showed up to meetings barefoot and bearded—didn't appear to lessen his zeal. Instead, his aggressiveness netted the help of several engineers, marketing firms, and venture capitalists.

The product of Wozniak's astounding engineering feats and Jobs' relentless ambition, Apple's mainstream computer, the Apple II, began selling like wildfire. The company mushroomed, with the Apple II bringing in huge profits. Media attention turned toward Silicon Valley, and Jobs, the master salesman, graced the cover of *Time* in 1982.

Jobs, however, is best known in the computer industry for leading the team that developed the boldly-designed computer used by millions today: the Apple Macintosh. During a demonstration of a prototype computer at the famed Xerox PARC, Jobs and other Apple employees were astounded by a computer that displayed graphical icons and pull-down menus in its operating system. The computer even allowed the user to issue commands from a small, wheeled device (a mouse). The demonstration's impact on the Apple team cannot be overestimated—Jobs scrambled to rewrite Apple's plan for its next computer, the Lisa, in order to accommodate the revolutionary ideas and logic of the Xerox PARC prototype. In its most basic description, the Lisa was the mother of the Macintosh. Targeted at corporate America, Lisa was a powerful computer destined to leapfrog its competition, but instead floundered in the marketplace mainly due to its hefty $10,000 price tag.

During this time, Jobs recruited Pepsi marketing executive John Sculley to join Apple as CEO. Jobs' management responsibility shifted to leading product development for a pint-sized version of Lisa, code-named Macintosh. Jobs' zealousness and management style drove the Macintosh team to sustained levels of intense work: seventy-plus hour weeks for months at a stretch became the norm. When later asked to explain their incredible work ethic, Macintosh team developers spoke of a sense of importance to their work, a messianic belief that the Macintosh would not only change computing, it would change the world.

Yet, after an initial spurt of sales to early adopters and yuppies, Macintosh sales lagged behind forecasts. Dissension in the nine-year-old company grew. Jobs and Sculley, once partners, became bitter enemies and attempted various power plays to remove each other. Politically more astute and agile than Jobs, Sculley won the showdown and Jobs was forced to retreat.

Jobs soon left the company with several key Apple employees in tow and started NeXT, his bid to revolutionize computing a second time. After a string of disappointing hardware product initiatives, NeXT boasted an estimated $60 million in yearly revenues in 1996—very respectable for a software company, but disappointing perhaps to those who expected nothing less than another rabbit hat trick and billion dollar revenues.

However, Steve Jobs still does magic. In an ironic twist to this Silicon Valley soap opera, Apple Computer decided to purchase NeXT for $400 million at the end of 1996. Why? Apple, by the end of 1996, was desperately struggling to revamp its own operating system and boost lagging sales. It needed a new vision, and chose NeXT—among several other potential companies—to fulfill that vision. Apple's reasons behind the purchase were widely speculated upon in the press, and many journalists had critical comments about Apple's strategy behind the acquisition—after all, NeXT only posted an annual profit once in the past four years, and was a market share laggard. Will NeXT—and Steve Jobs—be able to help save Apple? Only time will tell.

Fate rarely presents entrepreneurs more than one golden opportunity for commercial success. But Steve Jobs manages to defy the odds. Longing to enter computer animation, Jobs acquired the computer graphics division of Lucasfilm, renamed it *Pixar*, and helped shepherd it to a successful launch of a computer-generated feature film (*Toy Story*) and a public stock offering that pushed Jobs' estimated wealth well over the $500 million mark.

Yet, in the final analysis, Steve Jobs built a team of tremendously motivated and talented people who were able to truly change the world. All from a small company that started out of a suburban California garage.

We met with Steve Jobs at NeXT's corporate headquarters in Redwood City, California.

"You've got to be passionate about something!"

What talent do you think you consistently brought to Apple and bring to NeXT and Pixar?

I think that I've consistently figured out who really smart people were to hang around with. No major work that I have been involved with has been work that can be done by a single person, or two people, or even three or four people. Some people can do one thing magnificently, like Michaelangelo, and others make things like semiconductors or build 747 airplanes—that type of work requires legions of people. In order to do things well that can't be done by one person, you must find extraordinary people.

The key observation is that, in most things in life, the dynamic range between average quality and the best quality is, at most, two-to-one. For example, if you were in New York and compared the best taxi to an average taxi, you might get there 20 percent faster. In terms of computers, the best PC is perhaps 30 percent better than the average PC. There is not much difference in magnitude. Rarely you find a difference of 2 to 1. Pick anything.

But, in the field that I was interested in—originally, hardware design—I noticed that the dynamic range between what an average person could accomplish and what the best person could accomplish was 50 or 100 to 1. Given that, you're well advised to go after the cream of the cream. That's what we've done. You can then build a team that pursues the A+ players. A small team of A+ players can run circles around a giant team of B and C players. That's what I've tried to do.

So you think your talent is in recruiting?

It's not just recruiting. After recruiting, it's then building an environment that makes people feel they are surrounded by equally talented people and that their work is bigger than they are. The feeling that the work will have tremendous influence and is part of a strong, clear vision—all of those things. Recruiting usually requires more than you alone can do, so I've found that collaborative recruiting and having a culture that recruits the A players is the best way. Any interviewee will speak with at least a dozen people in several areas of this company, not just those in the area that he would work in. That way a lot of your A employees get broad exposure to the company, and—by having a company culture that supports them if they feel strongly enough—the current employees can veto a candidate.

That seems very time-consuming.

Yes, it is. We've interviewed people where nine out of ten employees thought the candidate was terrific, one employee really had a problem with the candidate, and therefore we didn't hire him. The process is hard, very time-consuming, and can lead to real problems if not managed right. But it's a very good way, all in all.

Yet, in a typical startup, a manager may not always have time to spend recruiting other people.

I disagree totally. I think it's the most important job. Assume you're by yourself in a startup and you want a partner. You'd take a lot of time finding the partner, right? He would be half of your company. Why should you take any less time finding a third of your company or a fourth of your company or a fifth of your company? When you're in a startup, the first ten people will determine whether the company succeeds or not. Each is ten percent of the company. So why wouldn't you take as much time as necessary to find all A players? If three were not so great why would you want a company where thirty percent of your people are not so great? A small company depends on great people much more than a big company does.

But, what about the need for speed when taking your product to market? Wouldn't recruiting in this manner take away time from getting your product to market quickly?

You'd better have great people or you won't get your product to market as fast as possible. Or, you might get a product to market really fast but it will be really clunky and nobody will buy it. There are no shortcuts around quality, and quality starts with people. Maybe shortcuts exist, but I'm not smart enough to have ever found any.

I spend 20 percent of my time recruiting even now. I spend a day a week helping people recruit. It's one of the most important things you can do.

If finding the A players is so important, how can you tell who is an A player and who isn't?

That's a very hard question. Ultimately there are two paths. If a candidate has been in the workplace for a while, you have to look at the results. There are people who look so good on paper and talk such a good story but have no results behind them. They can't point to breakthroughs or successful products that they shipped and played an integral part in. Ultimately the results should lead you to the people. As a matter of fact that's how I find great people. I look at great results and I find out who was responsible for them.

However, sometimes young people haven't had the opportunity yet to be in a position of influence to create such results. So here you must evaluate potential. It's certainly more difficult, but the primary attributes of potential are intelligence and the ability to learn quickly. Much of it is also drive and passion—hard work makes up for a lot.

When you recruit you're rolling the dice. No matter what, you're rolling the dice because you've only got an hour to assess the candidate. The most time I spend with somebody is an hour and I must then recommend whether we hire the person or not. Others will recommend, too, so I won't be the only one but I'll still have to throw my vote in the hat. Ultimately it comes down to your gut feeling. Your gut feeling gets refined as you hire more people and see how they do. Some you thought would do well don't and you can sense why. If you study it a bit you might say, "I thought this person was going to do well but I overlooked this aspect," or "I didn't think this person would do well but they did and here's why." As you hire people over time your gut instinct gets better and more precise.

Over time, my digging in during an interview gets more precise.

For example, many times in an interview I will purposely upset someone: I'll criticize their prior work. I'll do my homework, find out what
they worked on and say, "God, that really turned out to be a bomb.
That really turned out to be a bozo product. Why did you work on
that?" I shouldn't say this in your book, but the worse thing that someone can do in an interview is to agree with me and knuckle under.

What I look for is for someone to come right back and say,
"You're dead wrong and here's why." I want to see what people are
like under pressure. I want to see if they just fold or if they have firm
conviction, belief, and pride in what they did. It's also good every
once in a while to really piss somebody off in an interview to see how
they react because, if your company is a meritocracy of ideas, with
passionate people, you have a company with a lot of arguments. If
people can't stand up and argue well under pressure they may not do
well in such an environment.

*You mentioned how important it is to find good people, regardless of
the time to market issue. Yet, when you first started Apple it seemed as
if you were just hiring people as fast as you could.*

In the early days of Apple we were just trying to hire people that
knew more than we did about anything and that wasn't hard because
we didn't know a lot. The problem was not that we could find people
who knew more than we did. That was easy. The problem was that we
were pretty quick studies and before too long, we knew more than
they did and we'd ask questions that they couldn't answer because
they never really thought about it.

That was tough because we'd sometimes hire good people and
they didn't have the ability to grow as fast as we needed them to
grow, because in any young company your perspectives are changing
monthly as you learn more. People have to be able to change and
adapt and really be able to see things from new points of view. If they
get stuck in their own points of view, it gets very difficult.

What do you mean by getting stuck in their own points of view?

I'll give you an example. One of the reasons why Apple was successful was because we built the [computer] dealer channel. The dealer
channel did not exist before Apple built it. And, one of the things
Apple did to build the dealer channel was to finance it by extending
dealers credit when they were really not creditworthy.

So, we were extending credit, and when dealers were going

broke, we ate the cost of goods—that's part of the cost of building the channel. We quickly realized that we would have a lot less credit exposure if we could get our product to the dealer very fast because then they would not have to stock a lot of inventory. So, we created big distribution centers in several places around the country and dealers could get product shipped to them within twenty-four hours. This way, the dealer wouldn't have to stock much inventory, and we wouldn't have to extend them much credit.

After this system was established, I once asked Fred Smith [the CEO of Federal Express] how much would it cost to ship a Mac anywhere in the country directly from Apple to the customer within two days. He thought about it, did his calculations, and said about $27. I went back to Apple and analyzed our current distribution system which by this time took about three weeks from the factory to the customer. And, even worse, we found out that it cost us $57.

So, I proposed to our people that we completely eliminate the distribution warehouses, have FedEx just pick up Macs at the back of our factories, and have our computers link into Federal Express' tracking systems in order to eliminate paperwork and get the product from the factory to the customer within 48 hours. This way we would eliminate several hundred jobs and tons of computer systems, tons of bricks and mortar, while still getting the product to the customer three weeks sooner. But, I got my head shot off because people couldn't change their perspective.

Explain that a little more. What do you mean by "people couldn't change their perspective?"

Well, generally it's because people never know or forget what they're really doing—that is, what the benefit is to what they're really doing. Our distribution centers forgot that what they were really all about was getting product from Apple to its customers really fast. They thought they were about a whole lot of other things like personal relationships with the customer. They had taken over some sales functions, and it became a real mess. Eventually, the industry went the way of mail-order. Dell Computer was built on that model. Apple could have done what Dell did much sooner.

But, usually, people never think that much about what they're doing or why they do it. They just do it because that's the way it has been done and it works. That type of thinking doesn't work if you're growing fast and if you're up against some larger companies. You really have to out-think them and you have to be able to make those paradigm shifts in your points of view.

In addition to finding the right people, you also stated that building the environment of the company is important. What things can management do to create the right environment and culture of a young company?

Hewlett and Packard, of course, set the tone for the modern intellectual property-based company. They did such a good job of it that the rest of us have only built on their foundation. I'll explain this in a different way than they did. Most of the companies here create intellectual property. They are pure intellectual property companies. Some are different: Intel, for example, has billions of dollars in factories, but most companies don't.

Most of the companies in Silicon Valley succeed or fail based on their ability to have breakthrough ideas and implement those ideas. The implementation is primarily intellectual property—writing software and figuring out designs of one type or another. When your primary product is essentially bits on a disk or on a wire, your primary assets are human capital, not financial capital. And, since demand for people is greater than the supply, you must offer those people something more than a paycheck and stock options. You must offer them the ability to make larger decisions and to be a part of the core company. That involvement is what drives much of this fun.

For example, you want people to make key company decisions without you even knowing it. They'd better have access to most of the company's information, so you'd better have an open communication policy so that people can know just about everything, otherwise they will make important decisions without the right information. That would be really stupid. Generally technology companies are very open. Generally they are driven by the meritocracy of ideas, not by hierarchy. If there is someone really good four levels down—and you don't listen to them—they'll go somewhere else that will listen to them.

Hierarchy takes on a different meaning when people you work for are your coaches, not your bosses. If you're in Silicon Valley, you're your own boss because you don't have a contract. Silicon Valley does not work on contracts the way some industries do. If you don't like the way things are at one company, and if you're good, then you can leave anytime and go anywhere else. In fact, headhunters are calling you every week. All you have to do is take one of those calls and you're out of there. The whole power structure of an intellectual property-driven enterprise of good people is turned upside down. The CEO has the least power and the people with the most power are the hotshot individual contributors. They work as pure individual contributors and have more power than anybody because they come up with product.

Now, I'm exaggerating a little because middle managers are extraordinarily important—they hire and nurture these talented hotshots. Fundamentally, though, it would not be too distorted to say that the traditional corporate pyramid is completely inverted. That's the way it ought to be. Silicon Valley has pioneered the way that many businesses will need to be run as we enter the next century, where more and more companies are pure intellectual property interests.

That's nice from a theoretical standpoint. But from a practical standpoint, what does that mean? Does having access to information and "knowing just about everything" mean that a talented programmer can walk in your office and open your file cabinet whenever he wishes?

No. That wouldn't be appropriate because that's not showing respect for individuals and I'm an individual too. What it means is that employees can know things. We get the whole company together once a month and tell everybody everything that's going on. More companies are doing that but many don't.

And you also ask for suggestions and inputs.

Sure. That happens constantly. We'll stand up and say, "We just lost this order and here's why." Or, "We just won three orders and this is how the new product's coming, and this is how another product is slipping."

Whatever it might be: good news or bad news. And we talk about strategies. Once a year we go offsite for two days and bring the whole company, even the receptionists—we figure they might as well know what's going on too. We discuss company strategy: where we're going, where we're screwing up, and our plan for the coming year. We refocus and resynchronize everything once a year. We have heated discussions at those meetings, too. It costs a lot of money, but is incredibly valuable.

We've talked about the talent that you bring to companies. What do you think your weaknesses are when it comes to management?

I don't know. People are package deals; you take the good with the confused.

In most cases, strengths and weaknesses are two sides of the same coin. A strength in one situation is a weakness in another, yet often the person can't switch gears. It's a very subtle thing to talk about strengths and weaknesses because almost always they're the same thing.

My strength probably is that I've always viewed technology from a liberal arts perspective, from a human culture perspective. As such, I've always pushed for things that pulled technology in those directions by bringing insights from other fields. An example of that would be—with the Macintosh—desktop publishing: its proportionately spaced fonts, its ease of use. All of the desktop publishing stuff on the Mac comes from books: the typography, that rich feel that nobody in computers knew anything about. I think that my other strength is that I'm a pretty good judge of people and have the ability to bring people together around a common vision.

Well then, when are your strengths—judgment of character and liberal arts perspective—your weaknesses?

In certain cases my weaknesses are that I'm too idealistic. Realize that sometimes best is the enemy of better. Sometimes I go for "best" when I should go for "better," and end up going nowhere or backwards. I'm not always wise enough to know when to go for the best and when to just go for better. Sometimes I'm blinded by "what could be" versus "what is possible," doing things incrementally versus doing them in one fell swoop. Balancing the ideal and the practical is something I still must pay attention to.

In terms of going for the best, you have a widely held reputation of being extremely charismatic—someone who is always able to draw out the best in other people. How have you been able to motivate your employees?

Well, I think that—ultimately, it's the work that motivates people. I sometimes wish it were me, but it's not. It's the work. My job is to make sure the work is as good as it should be and to get people to stretch beyond their best. But it's ultimately the work that motivates people. That's what binds them together.

Yet, in the case of the Macintosh you got tremendous output from people. Regardless of the type of work, not everybody can elicit that type of commitment.

Well, I'm not sure I'd chalk that up to charisma. Part of the CEO's job is to cajole and beg and plead and threaten, at times—to do whatever is necessary to get people to see things in a bigger and more profound way than they have, and to do better work than they thought they could do.

When they do their best and you don't think it's enough, you tell them straight: "This isn't good enough. I know you can do better. You need to do better. Now go do better."

You must play those cards carefully. You must be right a lot of the time, because you're messing with people's lives. But that's part of the job. In the end, it's the environment you create, the coworkers, and the work that binds. The Macintosh team, if you talk to most of them—a dozen years since we shipped the product—most will still say that working on the Mac was the most meaningful experience of their lives. If we'd never shipped a product they wouldn't say that. If the product hadn't been so good they wouldn't say that. The Macintosh experience wasn't just about going to camp with a bunch of fun people. It wasn't just a motivational speaker. It was the product that everybody put their heart and soul into and it was the product that expressed their deep appreciation, somehow, for the world to see.

So, in the end it's the work that binds. That's why it's so important to pick very important things to do because it's very hard to get people motivated to make a breakfast cereal. It takes something that's worth doing.

Let's shift gears here. What should be the role of venture capitalists in starting new businesses?

In the old days venture capitalists helped a company a lot. They were mentors.

More so than today?

Yes. The reason is very simple. In the old days venture capitalists were people who had run businesses or major parts of businesses.

Don Valentine was the vice-president of marketing at National Semiconductor when he became a venture capitalist. Venture capitalists were people that had done substantial work in successful startup companies and were bringing their expertise and experience as much as their money.

But the industry grew so fast that it outstripped the ability to grow people of that caliber. Many VCs [venture capitalists] don't have that experience. They just bring money. Not that there's anything wrong with money, but it's unfortunate because things are very different now. I hear VCs sitting around arguing about whether to change CEOs or not. That's not what they ought to be talking about. They ought to be helping the companies make it.

So, if you were a young entrepreneur without money today, would you still go to them?

If you want to start a company and you're young, the best thing in the world is to find someone who's done it—who has experience and expertise and is looking to invest a little money. If that person happens to be a venture capitalist, so be it. If that person happens to be a private investor, so be it. If that person happens to be someone from a successful company that cashed in their stock options and is willing to invest a little bit, so be it. It doesn't matter what they call themselves. It matters who they are. It matters that they've had the experience.

What advice would you give someone interested in starting their own company?

A lot of people ask me, "I want to start a company. What should I do?" My first question is always, "What is your passion? What is it you want to do in your company?" Most of them say, "I don't know." My advice is go get a job as a busboy until you figure it out. You've got to be passionate about something. You shouldn't start a company because you want to start a company. Almost every company I know of got started because nobody else believed in the idea and the last resort was to start the company. That's how Apple got started. That's how Pixar got started. It's how Intel got started. You need to have passion about your idea and you need to feel so strongly about it that you're willing to risk a lot. Starting a company is so hard that if you're not passionate about it, you will give up. If you're simply doing it because you want to have a small company, forget it.

It's so much work and at times is so mentally draining. The hardest thing I've ever done is to start a company. It's the funnest thing, but it's the hardest thing, and if you're not passionate about your goal or your reason for doing it, you will give up. You will not see it through. So, you must have a very strong sense of what you want.

Whether it's baking bread or—

It doesn't matter what industry it is. There are very successful bakeries. There are very successful semiconductor companies. You name it, it doesn't really matter. What matters is that you feel very, very strongly about it. You have to need to run such a business and know you can do it better than anyone else. You have to really want it because it's going to take a lot of work, especially in the early stages.

What keeps you doing it? You could spend more time with family.

I come to Pixar and I come to NeXT every day. I come to them for two reasons: one, because what each company does is really great; and, two, because of the extraordinary people. I get to hang around many incredible people all day. That's why I do what I do.

I am, however, trying to lead a more balanced life. Since I have two kids, I certainly work much fewer hours and I've reduced my travel. If you don't find the balance, you won't have a family or you will miss it. Keeping things balanced is always a challenge.

Speaking of Pixar, how do you think the two industries—software and motion pictures—are similar? And how do they differ?

Well, the product life cycle is different.

Other than Pixar, almost everything else I've worked on in my life—an Apple II, for example—you can hardly find anymore. You won't be able to boot up a Macintosh in ten more years. Everything I've worked on in technology becomes the sediment layer for other things to build on top of. The Macintosh, for example, just advanced the culture at that time. Now, Windows has grabbed the baton and is running its leg of the relay. Later something else will.

In contrast, Pixar is putting something into culture that will renew itself with each generation of children. *Snow White* was re-released on video two years ago and sold over 20 million copies. It's sixty years old. I think people will be watching *Toy Story* in sixty years just the way they're watching *Snow White* now. The fact that the exact same movie will be watched 60 or 100 years from now is intriguing.

Speaking of the Mac, I wanted to talk a little bit about John Sculley. You've expressed, both privately and publicly, your dissatisfaction with him, and have even gone so far as to state that he destroyed Apple.

He did, yes.

If so, then what would have Steve Jobs done differently? What would Steve Jobs have done differently from John Sculley? Are we talking about not licensing its operating system, or allowing others to make compatibles?

No. It was much more profound than that.

For many years, Apple was about bringing a computer to everybody. It was about the personal computer revolution. It was about the products and the user's experience with those products. I was taught by some wise people that if you manage the top line of your company—your customers, your products, your strategy—then the bottom line will follow. But if you manage the bottom line of the company and forget about the rest, you'll eventually hit the wall because you'll take your eyes off the prize.

At Apple, the top management basically got very corrupt—starting with John—in several ways. They got corrupt about their purpose and became very financially driven instead of product- and customer-driven. They became financially corrupt and started self-dealing: there were a lot of company Mercedes, company planes, and company houses. Who am I to say, but my guess is that if somebody plowed through that stuff it would border on criminal. Previous to that, Apple had been a very democratic, egalitarian place. No one had palatial offices. There weren't fat cats at the top.

The most important part of this corruption was that the values of the company changed. They changed from the conviction of making the best computers in the world to the conviction of making money—a very subtle thing, really. This, and the fact that most of the people who made the breakthrough products soon left the company, was what destroyed Apple.

Many new people joined Apple. But, it was as if they boarded a rocket ship as it was leaving the launch pad and they thought they made the rocket ship rather than having just been passengers, which is all they really were. All these passengers were convinced that they made the rocket ship. That was fine until the company needed a new rocket ship. Yet, Apple has, up to this point, not been able to make one. They tried with Newton. That was a fiasco and they're still on the same rocket ship. They needed a new one years ago, but the culture doesn't exist to know how to build rocket ships.

I'll try to muster it in one sentence. Apple had a wonderful set of values that was based on, in many ways, what Hewlett-Packard did. We copied a lot and tried to build upon it. Our values were about building the best computers in the world and when those values changed to the value of "the reason we make computers is to make a lot of money," many things started to change, subtly and not so subtly. The kind of people that flourished in the old value system didn't flourish in the new one. A different set of people flourished. The biggest manifestation of these changed values was that before we wanted as many people as possible to use our products. We didn't call it market share in those days, but it was.

Apple's greatest mistake, in my opinion, is not that it did or didn't license their technology in the late '80s. Apple's biggest mistake was that it got immensely greedy. Apple priced the product so high that it didn't go for market share and left a giant umbrella for the PC industry. We originally weren't on that trajectory. The reason we built the Mac factory was to get the Mac down to $1,000 someday, but instead they sold it for much, much more. I think Apple could now have a 35 percent market share had management cared about people using Apple computers instead of making $400 million a year in profits.

It's what you care about. An organization with talented people will definitely adjust itself to the value structure expressed at the top. People who were better for one value structure, when it changes, will leave. And other people will come in. You can change an organization in a big way in five years. That's part of what happened at Apple. They hired a stream of mediocre people, just one after another after another.

Speaking of great products, what do you think the next great products of this industry are going to be? What's its future?

To be honest, I have no idea.

All you can see are the plate tectonic trends. The trend is that computers will move from primarily being a computational device to primarily a communications device. We've known that was coming. The internet is certainly doing it on a larger scale than some people had imagined. But what this all means yet I don't know. The internet was around for a long time before the World Wide Web made it more approachable, and yet the World Wide Web is still a very simplistic thing. I think there's room for a lot more breakthroughs. I think when they happen they might spread very quickly, much like the World Wide Web did, meaning that in a period of five years things could be very different. But it's hard to say exactly what they're going to be. It's very hard.

2

T. J. RODGERS

Cypress Semiconductor

THE IMPORTANCE OF VISION, ACCORDING TO THE GENERAL

T. J. Rodgers is founder, president, and CEO of Cypress Semiconductor. Based in San Jose, CA, Cypress is an international supplier of integrated circuits (i.e., chips) for a range of markets including high-performance computers, telecommunications, instrumentation, and military systems.

Thurman J. Rodgers, or T. J. as he is known, went to Dartmouth College where he graduated as Salutatorian with a double major in physics and chemistry. Rodgers attended Stanford on a Hertz fellowship, where he earned a Ph.D. in 1975 in electrical engineering. While at Stanford, Rodgers invented and patented VMOS (Vertical Metal-Oxide Semiconductor) technology, which he later sold to American Microsystems (AMI). He managed the MOS memory design group at AMI from 1975 to 1980 and then moved to Advanced

Micro Devices (AMD), where he led their static RAM product group.

In 1983, after dissatisfaction with AMD's management, T. J. left to found Cypress. Four years later, the company went public. It now has annual revenues of over $600 million and employs over 1,500 people.

Part of Cypress' financial success can be ascribed to its culture. Cypress is a company based on five core values—which Rodgers proceeded to explain to us in detail. Rodgers takes pride in fostering these values at Cypress, and has also written *Harvard Business Review* articles and a book, *No Excuses Management*, about them.

Rodgers' reputation as one of Silicon Valley's most outspoken CEOs is well deserved. Whether the issue is U.S. immigration policy, workplace diversity, or Cypress' competition, Rodgers delivers his opinions with a brash, no-nonsense style that some find abhorrent and others refreshingly honest.

In one recent episode, Rodgers received a letter from a Catholic nun requesting that he make Cypress' board of directors more diverse. His response, a blistering six-page letter reprinted in the *Wall Street Journal*, bluntly informed Sister Doris that her advice wasn't needed.

We met with T. J. at Cypress' headquarters. Sparse and modestly appointed, his office's only lavish accouterment is the Frederic Remington sculpture on a nearby bookcase—a frontier-era cowboy bravely riding atop a defiant, bucking bronco.

"Large companies must be screwing a lot of stuff up to lose when they're that big."

Why did you leave AMD to start your own company?

Actually, my mother asked me that. Her basic question was—rephrasing it negatively from my perspective—"Now that you're in the rat race and can scramble up the political ladder at Advanced Micro Devices, why give up the sure opportunities and start your own company?"

I wanted to start a company since I graduated from college. It was one of my life goals, stated at age 21, that I would start a company by age 35. Why do people actually start their own companies? The standard entrepreneurial answer is frustration. You see a company running poorly; you see that it could be a whole lot better.

Like the freshman Congressman who's been around for six months, you realize that the other guys really aren't that good. All of a sudden you understand that you could go build something bigger and more important than where you are. That's a big deal.

Does the idea have to be original?

No. I think that premise is total bullshit. If you look at Hewlett-Packard, their first two products were automatic urinal flushers and bowling pin setters—those are hardly unique ideas. In our case, we both did and did not have a unique idea.

Our business plan was to attack the big companies by building a technically superior product: memory—RAM. I'm a technologist. I have a Ph.D. in electrical engineering from Stanford and my specialty is transistor physics. While at AMD, I saw CMOS [complementary metal-oxide semiconductor process technology used to make integrated circuits, or chips].

CMOS had existed for a decade when I was at Stanford in 1974. I knew by having roomed with one of the people who did early work on CMOS that it was clearly the technology of the future. I realized in 1974 it was going to happen. In 1979 I knew exactly how to do it, and at AMD I was prevented from doing it by internal politics, by superiors who had not a clue about technology.

I looked at the semiconductor business, saw wonderful opportunities, calculated that I could attack with a RAM product that was twice as fast. Twice as fast, half the power, half the chip size. If you make a part for two dollars that you sell for four dollars, and I can make it for a dollar and sell it for eight, then I win.

I saw exactly how to do that and I concluded the same thing the Japanese did about the same time in 1979: the American semiconductor industry was really weak; the powerhouses, Intel and Advanced Micro Devices, were arrogant. They were riding a wave they no longer had earned, and they could be taken apart by superior technology.

The balloon was ready to burst. I saw it and the Japanese saw it. I jumped in and attacked existing products. Ours was really a

Japanese-style attack of superior technology. We also had pretty good manufacturing and always have had. So there was no whiz-bang idea.

Why didn't AMD want to do CMOS if it was a better technology?

I came to AMD to run their NMOS technology. NMOS is half of CMOS. I figured out that there was no fundamental reason for CMOS being slow; it could be very fast. All of a sudden, I was looking at the prospect of attacking the fastest technology with the lowest-power technology that was also cheaper. I explained the idea and AMD hired a group to do CMOS research and development. Those guys were political cretins, their boss was a moron, and they proceeded to screw up their implementation big time.

I explained why they screwed it up. I wrote the four-page memo explaining technically why they had missed the mark. Basically, they were Intel copycats. Intel had tried the same thing and screwed it up. AMD had assumed that, because Intel couldn't do it, they couldn't do it. So, the argument was about authority and turf as opposed to transistors, electrons, and pico-seconds and pico-farads. It infuriated me.

I had been very successful in the NMOS group. I developed a $25 million RAM business for AMD that was very, very capable. We were taking market share when I ran the group. And yet they refused to let me have CMOS. It was only after I had decided to leave that continued failure by the CMOS guys caused the group to report to me.

At that point in time I wanted to take apart the little political clique that I didn't like. Then I was disallowed to manage the group the way I wanted. So I argued with subordinates on technology issues, and they would threaten to run to daddy [AMD CEO Jerry Sanders] if I didn't do what they wanted. If you think about it, any billion-dollar company that has so much money to spend on R&D should be unassailable. It should crunch little companies like bugs. But the large companies routinely cannot crunch little companies, so something's got to be wrong. Large companies must be screwing a lot of stuff up to lose when they're that big. That's how it was inside AMD.

Do you think that that's why Cypress was able to handle competition as a small firm—because Intel and AMD were not as technically proficient?

It's not that they weren't as proficient. Rather it was because they were really screwed up. AMD suffered through the early 1980s and never, ever got CMOS. Jerry Sanders was years late getting into CMOS, precisely because of what I just said. He'd have been in CMOS and a lot richer years earlier had he let me run it based on merit, which he didn't because he's not a technologist and doesn't understand. He delegated the decision down the chain of command and the next guy didn't understand either. My life was too short for that kind of crap. They weren't not proficient; they were pathetic. That's why the Japanese kicked their asses.

They're now competent, and that's why they shoved the Japanese back. That's the entire thing; it's got nothing to do with MITI, government subsidies, or any of that bullshit. Basically, incompetent companies got beat. To their credit, AMD decided not to lose. They changed, started doing quality improvement and statistical process control. I won't say as good as the Japanese, but they're so close in manufacturing the difference is irrelevant relative to the huge advantage they have in invention, which the Japanese don't have.

How are you different in terms of product innovation? How does Cypress listen to an employee with a good product idea any better than AMD did to you?

That's a good question. People have come to me with ideas that I thought were bad ideas. Some people have left the company to pursue ideas that I thought were bad ideas. The difference is that I'm involved. I'm involved in personally evaluating new technology initiatives. I'm a technology junkie. I understand that technology is what moves our industry. I view technology not as a threat—the story I just told—but as an opportunity. Therefore I personally get involved in it.

It's kind of reversed here at Cypress. My VP of R&D is, in effect, a manufacturing person in research and development. His check partly depends upon putting the technologies into production. Meanwhile I sit in the room saying, "That's a great idea. Why don't we do this and do that?" The VP of R&D sits there with white knuckles thinking, "God, he's going to have me make something really risky." I'm the force trying to pull more technology into the company and the bureaucracy has to make those things happen.

I evaluate the technology; I am very open to new ideas. I evaluate every new product in this corporation. I spend three hours a week in an open forum where I bring in our manufacturing people, marketing people, applications engineers, product-line managers, and technical design persons. In that forum we listen to any product proposal that comes from anywhere. If you get it approved you're on your way. The criteria for approval aren't as simple as: "Gee, it's a funky idea, so let's go spend a million dollars." Nonetheless, if you've got a good idea and you're willing to come to the meeting and withstand some tough scrutiny, you can get an idea launched.

In 1992 sales were down and you had to move away from your 100 percent American content pledge. You moved manufacturing to Thailand. Was the answer entirely evident that moving manufacturing offshore was the right thing?

The answer was entirely evident, and the debate in the company was everybody against me. I was the bad guy in that case. So what went wrong in 1992?

First of all, we had an all-American strategy. And all-American meant we manufactured here. We also had a niche product strategy, which meant we had 5,000 product/package combinations. We also had a bunch of military business. So I fought the decision. Keeping manufacturing in the U.S. was $17 million a year in added cost. From the time we started the company, when the theory was semi-valid, we were probably always a 30 percent profitability company.

We said, "We're doing great and would have been better had we not had the burden of U.S. manufacturing all along." What went wrong was that the competition automated. So they had one-dollar-per-hour people running robots, when I had two twelve-dollar-an-hour people running robots. Point one.

Point two is that the world went offshore for assembly and testing, which is low-tech—i.e., you can do it anywhere. I'm talking about injection molding with a high-tech plastic: you basically melt it and spill it in mold.

When the industry went overseas, the East gained a core competency in assembly and testing. America was behind offshore. Not only was I running at a disadvantage on labor costs, I was running against management cultures in the Far East that had developed Statistical Process Control for the backend, which is unheard of in America. I finally got pushed over the brink by my board to abandon the all-American strategy.

You got pushed by your board?

Yes. They were all over me.

The board drove the decision?

The board were old National Semiconductor guys; they put plants all over the world, they knew exactly how to do it, and they were all over my ass. I kept pushing back on them. I was making 23 percent profit.

What did they want me to do? Walk across the street and say, "Congratulations four hundred of you. You've done a great job and we've made record profits. But record profits aren't enough. I'm laying you all off so I can move offshore to make more profit." Then I'd look at the board and say, "Why don't one of you guys do that speech, because I'm not particularly up for it." In retrospect they were absolutely right. If you think about it economically, an all-American strategy is stupid. You can't swim upstream against the world economy.

It just doesn't happen.

Countries can't do it, let alone companies. Now that I've analyzed it more, the all-American strategy is contrary to my basic economic principles. And those principles are that *there are no safe harbors— the only safe harbor is competency.* Competency at doing something. Knowledge.

Knowledge is equal to profit. It's very simple. When you can't justify something by being confident and knowledgeable and when somebody else can perform the same task more cheaply and efficiently, you'll let them do it and focus on what you know and do well.

The second issue was after having attacked the fat, arrogant major companies successfully, we went ahead and did exactly what they did: we read our own newspaper clips.

I mounted all those clippings on my wall and got arrogant. In manufacturing we improved from 1983 quality to 1985 quality by 1992. The other guys, whose asses we had previously kicked, went from 1985 to 1992 in real-time. And all of a sudden I woke up one day and Intel and AMD were no longer patsies.

Our manufacturing was behind. That was a cultural problem because our attitude at manufacturing was, "We are Cypress. How can we be behind?" They couldn't tolerate saying, "We're behind, we're getting beat, and we've got to change." We brought in a change agent.

Now that you've seen almost every semiconductor company struggle at some point, is there one that you admire most?

Micron Technology, because I'm a manufacturing and technology guy. It's a sucker answer not to say Intel because they in effect invented the personal computer and da-da-dah. But the fact is I like Micron.

I had the all-American problem; solving the all-American problem was simple. I'll never forget it. One of my vice-presidents said, "Even if we do everything to improve efficiency, we're going to be behind our competition by X million dollars a year, and we can't afford it any longer."

I remember my head switched with a click. "Okay, you're right. We've got to change." So after five years, we changed. In the middle of a quarter, we peeled 50 testers in assembly molds, one at a time and made sure that they were up and running seven days later in Thailand. I can now make a RAM cheaper than any Japanese company. Maybe Micron can make a RAM cheaper, maybe not. But I believe we can do it cheaper than anybody. The Japanese have been pushed back out of the SRAM business.

How much and since when?

Since 1985. That was the crisis and it required a transformation of the corporation into a worldwide company—a rededication to benchmarking and learning in manufacturing. And now, we've diversified a lot of stuff. In seven days, our first RAM will take off from our Bangalore, India design center. We'll find out if they can make RAMs. We trained them in our Mississippi design center. We're now diversifying everything.

It seems like you're in a pretty attractive industry—lots of demand, lots of barriers to entry.

It's true. In one way, it's brutal. It's brutal in that the difference between a ridiculous plus or minus two percent learning curve compounded over three years will put you out of business. But once you can live in that world and you require change and compare the rate of change to competitors, then what you say is true and it's getting more true.

Right now we're buying back $50 million worth of our own stock, because Wall Street doesn't understand that. The herd has gotten afraid and they're running in the wrong direction. A year from today, if you call me up, I will have bought $50 million worth of our stock, and I will have sold it back to Wall Street for $100 million. I will have made $50 million because I understand the industry and they don't.

Knowledge is profit. They're going in the wrong direction, big time. The industry this year is $146 billion. Five years ago it was fifty. Five years before that it was seventeen. Five years before that it was about four. The industry has gone from four to $150 billion in fifteen years. In 2000, we're looking at $350 billion—2.7 Intels, 2.7 Cypress', 2.7 Japan Incs., and 2.7 Koreas.

You can imagine. By the year 2005 the number is $850 billion, a factor of six over the next ten years. I'm closer to the six times bigger industry, adding five of our industries on top of what we've got, than I am to when Cypress started. And I absolutely agree with you that semiconductors are becoming king. We're headed to the era of the chip industry sucking up the systems industry—a good chunk of it. The first to go was the personal computer industry. I see the chip industry growing astronomically and I see the manufacturing component of the industry being very important.

What will dominate the semiconductor industry in the future? SRAMs, flash memory?

I've stopped looking at the market in terms of products. If you take ten-year looks at the semiconductor industry, what's important? Change.

The main thing is to be able to make millions of transistors, hook them up and make something useful out of them, and you have to be flexible enough to use different technologies and make different kinds of products. Cypress will have one or more drivers of our technology so that if the SRAM business softens for some reason, we won't be left out in the cold from having a specialized little niche.

We can take sand and make a million transistor things. That's what we're about. And today they contain SRAMs. They might not in the future. That'll be a gradual, half-decade kind of change. It won't be precipitous. We won't go out of business if SRAMs wind down but we might hurt for a couple years.

You're a wealthy guy. What keeps you at Cypress?

There are three options for me. I've been asked to run for Congress and I turned it down; I was asked to run against Norm Manetta, that lame-duck Democratic master of pork. Why would I want to be a wealth allocator with no value-added—or negative value-added—when I'm a wealth creator?

Why would I want to commute to Washington, D.C., and deal

with political morons when I can run a semiconductor company? I only made a paltry $40 million starting Cypress. Why don't I do it right? Why don't I, for example, take my $40 million, fund a company myself, do an IPO with a $200 million valuation and own 60 percent of the stock? That'd be better—a Bill Gates kind of number.

I don't know. I already have enough money to buy a better car than the two-year-old Honda Accord that I have, but I really don't want to. If I had a better car I would feel terrible about beating it to death commuting and frying it in the parking lot. I don't use most of my money so I don't need more money. I've got plenty of money. Why don't I get into the big leagues? Why don't I do what George Fisher did? He's a Ph.D.; he's a smart guy. I can wait for one of the names that the world recognizes, Kodak, to get sick and then take it over to see if I could turn it around.

Well, Cypress is going to be a $2 billion company in 2000, and we're going to be five or more billion in 2005. Right where I am I can run a big company if I stay in the chair for ten more years. Also, it'll be my kind of folks here. I don't have to come in and make the company unsick; I won't have to deal with layers of bureaucrats or having my department managers going to New York.

Then what's the big job? Being President of the United States? Think of the corporal punishment. Assuming I could do that job, which I can't, I'd be forced to campaign all over the United States, enduring mudslinging fights with competitors about nothing and kowtow to the press.

Or to special interest groups.

Right. Having to make life-threatening decisions: will I take money from tobacco or not? Will I take money from the American Trial Lawyers association? Americans hate politicians and they've come to hate the President. Look at the President of the United States and the snide implications and the rude questions he receives. It's awesome that he should have to put up with that kind of crap, but he does. He allows it and they hate him. Generically. Not just Clinton, but they hate him.

People around here don't hate me. They understand what I stand for; they choose to be here. The ones who choose to be here, I work with; we have fun. That's why I'm here. Then you have to formalize why other people are here. That's the statement of purpose, which is a boil-down of the core values. So then you say, "Am I here to be a static-RAM guy?" If you don't want your life's work to be something that might be obsolescent in five years, no. "Am I here to be a chip guy?" Yes. "Do we make the best chips in the world?" Yes.

Tell us about the role of culture, values, and vision in your company.

I found out something about corporate culture, à la Collins and Porras [Jim Collins and Jerry Porras, authors of *Built to Last: Visionary Habits of Successful Companies*]: the importance of having a set of core values.

They describe a methodology for establishing a company's core values and culture. In the past core values have been turned over to the witch doctors, touchy-feely psychologists, earth-shoe wearing, global-driving, granola-eaters that want self-esteem to be the major aspect of every corporation. Self-esteem here is defined as, "Speak nice, talk nice, everybody happy all the time," right until you go out of business.

Collins and Porras reduced that core value-setting process to an objective methodology which people can buy into. You realize, in retrospect, that cultures are real, they're powerful, and they work. One of our core values in this corporation is, "We tell the truth." It's an absolute core value. If you want to get your ass blown out of this company all you have to do is be a slimeball and a liar and a politician and you immediately are *persona non grata*.

When did vision and values become important to Cypress?

After 1992. This was a remedial action as part of the 1992 "figure-out-who-you-are" situation. Another problem we had in 1992 was that our original business plan clearly specified that we were going to be a high-tech company. Our chips were going to be smaller, faster, and better than the other guys' chips, and we were going to take our competitors on and blow them up. But we lost the edge in 1992 because at $250 million in revenues we niched out and stalled. The niches had created such daunting manufacturing, sales, and marketing tasks that our people were stretched extremely thin.

Even though our employees worked their butts off, they couldn't do a quality job. The fact that I demanded a quality job meant that I was butting heads with people all the time. The fact that we weren't doing well financially meant that I couldn't afford the resources to build resources. We fundamentally had to change niches.

People said, "If we don't make the fastest chips in the world, then who are we?" I kept presenting the business plan over and over and over. I kept showing them what we were making, why we were making it, who we were competing against, what we were doing and I kept getting feedback that we didn't have a vision for the company. And it really pissed me off because I kept telling them what we were going to do. But it didn't substitute for a vision. In my mail one day came a paper from this prof that I never heard of at Stanford, Jim Collins. The paper rattled around in my briefcase for two months and then I read it. There is a line in *Apocalypse Now*. Have you seen it?

Yes.

Heavy flick. There's a line where Marlon Brando talks about a vision, a piercing vision where he suddenly saw through the clouds, and he said, "It was like a diamond bullet hitting me right between the eyes."

I read the paper and I said, "This is it. This is the diamond bullet."

Previously, I had gone into this touchy-feely realm with witch doctors. When you tread in this land, it's loaded with witch doctors. All of a sudden I saw an objective, bottoms-up, fact-knowledge-reason method for saying who we are. It was "valueless" in that it didn't espouse one set of values or another. You didn't have to pick up Tom Peters' book which says that if you do A, B, and C you'll be a successful company—worthless things like that. With the Collins and Porras book, you define who you are, how great companies know who they are and who they are not. That's really the big message in the book.

So, our five core values of the corporation are:

- We're here to win.
- Cypress people are only the best.
- We "do what's right for Cypress."
- We make our numbers—no excuses.
- We make what we sell—we're not a storefront.

Core value number one: We're competitive, we enjoy the game. Our competitors like Andy Grove are people who can't be disregarded—we made that mistake once. Jerry Sanders as well. We blew him off as a salesman. Guess what? Jerry's still there and AMD is now a $2 billion company.

In 1993, one question arose when the finance group came back and said, "We're *not* here to win. How can we be winning when we just got our ass kicked in 1992? We're not winning, we're recovering. We don't know if we'll recover to preeminence, or if we'll just be another company." The fact was, our then-current performance was different from one of our core values. So, we rephrased the value as "We will not tolerate losing."

If winning is *not* a core value, then you just say "Shit happens." You bumble along with mediocre performance until you get acquired or get fired. But if winning is a core value, then you have a visceral reaction that you're violating a core value, like somebody's lying to you. If you know someone's lying, you don't tolerate it. You call them on it right there on the spot. We will not tolerate losing.

Looking at our core values, can I say we do them right all the time? Absolutely not. Are there people who don't work hard at Cypress? Probably a few. What I can tell you is that not working hard isn't too well tolerated here. On the third night that someone walks out at eight o'clock, he will approach the person who left at 4:30 that previous afternoon, and ask, "Hey. Why don't we get this done tonight before we leave together?"

The culture itself works on that. This is how we handle a dissonance between actual performance and core values. Our products and technologies compete head-on with the best in the world. The fact that we're right there with those big Japanese companies, their accomplishments per person—it's extraordinary.

Conventional wisdom states that the semiconductor industry will consolidate like the automobile industry and will be left with a Big Three. Bullshit. There are 200 companies, and the last time I looked, the important, sexy companies that everybody was talking about were all new ones.

Like NexGen, and C-Cubed.

NexGen—Jerry Blowhard [Sanders of AMD, which acquired NexGen] is the primary guy discussing the consolidation of the industry, yet it's he who has to bail his company out by purchasing a startup. He bought it at a ratio of 45 times revenue. I love it!

We create an environment for *individuals* to win in business so we recognize not teamwork, but individuals. I have a vision which may be as screwed up as the previous one, but I have come to conclude that the P&L statement and the balance sheet are the most powerful tools of measurement we have. I really believe that. All of my little bonus plans are dramatically inferior to the P&L statement, which is time-tested and breadth-tested.

With little bonus plans, you find out, you're incentivizing things you didn't need to incentivize. For example, you feed hungry people to make yourself feel better that hungry people are fed. The downside is you incentivize not working. By subsidizing not working, pretty soon you find out that, when at first you intended to feed and help a few hundred people, you're now supporting millions. I see those unintended consequences around here all the time. So I decided to keep it simple: P&Ls that everybody understands and can deal with.

Core value number two: Cypress people are only the best. This is the first thing that everybody tells me in every meeting. Cypress people are smart and work hard. We don't allow things to languish. We tell the truth. We make no excuses. We value detailed knowledge, logic, and reason.

The flip-side is we deplore corporate politicians. The way you can tell you're dealing with a politician is straightforward, even if you're in an area in which you're technically inept. All you need to do is ask a simple question and you'll get something back that logically just doesn't fit. When you ask a series of logical questions, you're building a box. Pretty soon the person answering the questions is in the box. And just when you're going to put side six on the cube, the politician hops out. So you start to build a new box. After you've built your third box, you suddenly understand you're dealing with a politician.

Politicians are overstanders; they've got something they want. They've got a philosophy, a belief set. Your belief set can be Christianity, it can be political correctness, it can be liberal politics—a set of things you believe in that you don't require data of in order to support. You just simply believe it. Once you come from that point of view, you try to fit the world into your balloon.

But electrons don't understand that. They don't understand beliefs. They only understand reality and the laws of physics, and therefore people in the electron-moving business inevitably get screwed if they deal from a belief point of view. For example, "America Forever"—that expression is a belief. There's nothing to support that statement bottom-up. You get screwed when you have a belief that's not rooted in the basics.

Core value number three. We do what's right for Cypress. It doesn't mean you sleep here on weekends, but what it does mean is you're a company owner. We give you stock. We have the highest dilution percent per year, due to employee shares, of any company.

We do about six percent per year. We give stock to everybody, and we give it every year.

No matter where they are on the chain?

No matter where they are on the chain. Our shares are highly discriminatory, but there is at least a little bit for everybody, so everybody watches the ticker tape.

They care.

Right. So we choose wins over looking good. We reward personal initiative. Go out and kick ass, take names, make it happen and you will get the credit for having done it. We're loyal and fair to our people.

Core value number four: We make our numbers. We set aggressive quantitative goals. We set aggressive quantitative goals in all areas and we achieve them. It's our fetish for numbers.

What kind of quantitative goals can you set in "soft" areas like marketing or Human Resources?

I can tell you the first pass yield—the success percentage of every sales area manager—in selling each of our fourteen product lines. I could tell you what he was selling well, what he wasn't selling well, and 99,000 other metrics. I could go into our tax department and I could show you Pareto plans for reducing our tax rate, piece by piece.

I can go to HR and show you metrics for training. Again, we set goals that are quantitative, we set goals that improve, and we compare ourselves to that and go beat on it. It's a mathematical version of kaizen—Japanese continual improvement. It's all over the company.

The alternative is to have a floater who has no goals, no objectives, and says, "What? Who am I? Why am I here? What am I doing?" So we constantly improve. The goals get tougher all the time. For example, we used to track revenue-per-employee. We used to drive it up. We then ran into the problem where a VP chooses not to hire a $100,000 heavy-hitter, and chooses instead to hire two college grads and spend a lot of time training them. Does he get hit by a factor of two in revenue-per-employee? Maybe he shouldn't, given that the two college grads might be cheaper than the one heavy-hitter. We've gone to a new metric though we still report revenue-per-employee because it's a metric that all semiconductor companies are compared by. We now use dollars of revenue per dollar of indirect labor cost.

Our costs are the best in the world. We don't tolerate waste. That is a contrast for those of us who worked at big companies and saw a lot of waste.

Like your experience at AMD?

AMD has always been catastrophic. When AMD was in the throes of laying people off—blood spewing all over—the board of directors was a pocket board. I don't have a pocket board. My board will kick me in the ass routinely, which I appreciate. For example, if I'm screwing up—maintaining that we only do manufacturing in America, regardless of the facts—then it's their job to hammer on me. Jerry's board is the other way around. Jerry does what Jerry wants.

For example, it is rumored—I haven't verified this—that he has a driver and bodyguard in Northern California, and a driver and bodyguard in Southern California. He's got either a Rolls or Bentley in each place. He was asked to give up the Southern California or Northern California car, and he said no. This was happening during the bottom of AMD's business.

Was it a company car?

Yes. Company car, company bodyguard, company driver. There was also the week-long Riviera trip that Jerry takes. One of our directors was walking along the harbor in Cannes—he was taking his son to Europe for the first time. They see this incredible yacht with twin Ferrari engines in the back, and decide to nose around. They get to the back of the boat and there's Jerry with his daughter and his wife—who are both about the same age—and some other dolly hanging on him. Of course AMD's board of directors get invited and he cruises around the islands during vacation.

I've also heard—no verification—that this is written off as a business expense. We don't do that here. We sometimes go out of our way to show that we don't do it.

Core value number five: We make what we sell. We like to make things. Basically, we're proud of our technology and products. Our designs are excellent and our designers are extremely disciplined, relative to the typical flaky Silicon Valley company. We like to manufacture stuff and we like to make it in volume. We have good product quality.

Although I can't tell you Cypress stands for quality, I can tell you that our fetish for numbers and logical reasoning causes our product to be of high quality. Of the thirteen preferred vendors at AT&T, we're ranked number one in quality. We're the only one of the thirteen with under a billion dollars in revenue.

You said that you don't really care about quality, and yet you've also stated that, "We make the best chips in the world." Are you saying quality's really an end result of your working hard?

What I'm saying is, we do not have a culture which says, "Quality's what I'm about." Let's suppose that Ford's little motto turns out to be a core value.

Quality is job one—

—or has been inspired to be a core value. Hypothetically, you'd walk up to a person in the Ford assembly line and say, "What do you do?" He wouldn't say, "We bang out one car every second." Instead he'd say, "Quality is job one." That's what would motivate him because he's prioritized it really high. Quality, in this case, is defined as average outgoing quality, as opposed to the broader TQM concept of corporate quality.

But, if you asked our people what they do, they'd say, "We make the lowest cost wafers in the world. We make the hottest transistors in the world. My RAM is faster than anybody's RAM. My RAM has a smaller chip than anybody else's RAM. We can ship into any socket, anywhere in the world, at any price and still make a profit better than our competitors." They would say all of those things, but they wouldn't say, "We emphasize quality manufacturing. It's the most important thing we do." It just isn't in the woodwork. Nonetheless, the way we operate produces a high quality product.

3

GORDON EUBANKS

Symantec

BRANDS AND BANDS

Gordon Eubanks is president and CEO of Symantec Corporation, a software manufacturer. Symantec is best known for making the Norton Utilities, but also develops other desktop software products including programming languages (Symantec C++) and communications tools (WinFax Pro).

Eubanks' route to the CEO slot was circuitous. Though he had no particular interest in electronics during childhood, Eubanks recalls childhood dreams of one day owning a computer—which, in the late 1950s, bordered on megalomania. He settled on studying engineering at Oklahoma State University and graduated with a Bachelor of Science degree in electrical engineering in 1968.

From 1970 to 1979, Eubanks served in the United States Navy as a commissioned marine officer. During his tenure as a submarine officer, Eubanks was part of what he likes to call the "Hunt for Red October stuff." Although his team never stole any Russian submarines, Eubanks is very fond of his Navy experience. He describes it as a high-pressure management environment where accountability was key. This sense of accountability evolved into what his colleagues describe as an intense focus and drive to succeed.

As a master's degree candidate in computer science at the Naval Postgraduate School, Eubanks had to choose a thesis advisor. His selection: the combative, but legendary Gary Kildall, founder of Digital Research [not to be confused with Ken Olsen's Digital Equipment Corporation] and the inventor of the CPM operating system.

During his work with Kildall, Eubanks created EBASIC, one of the first widely used "Basic" language tools for Kildall's CPM. EBASIC evolved into CBASIC, one of the first commercially successful languages for personal computers.

Eubanks, who describes the software industry as "one of the greatest opportunities of the 20th century," started Compiler Systems Inc., whose first major product was CBASIC. The company was moderately successful, and Eubanks sold the company to Digital and became one of Digital's vice-presidents.

Dissatisfied with Digital's management, Eubanks left again in 1983, and founded C&E (Coleman & Eubanks) software with Dennis Coleman, a Stanford business school professor. In 1984, C&E purchased Symantec, and Eubanks has been president of Symantec ever since.

One of the reasons for Symantec's growth to a half-billion-dollar company is Eubanks' cookiemonster strategy: Symantec's purchase of more than 20 companies gives it access to top quality people and products, which it has deftly used to diversify its product line.

Another aspect of Symantec's strategy is its close partnership with Microsoft. Never ascribing to membership in Silicon Valley's "We-Hate-Bill" club, Eubanks and Symantec have adroitly taken advantage of the relationship by creating products that complement those of Microsoft. Because creating utility software requires a deep understanding of the operating system, Symantec and Microsoft developers work closely together to ensure the interoperability of their products: Microsoft developers inform Symantec of anticipated changes to Microsoft's current operating system, and Symantec adapts its software.

Gordon Eubanks was one of the most approachable, down-to-earth executives we interviewed. Eschewing technical jargon or trendy management-speak, Eubanks' mantra is simple: to make products that add value to the customer.

We met with Eubanks at Symantec's worldwide headquarters in Cupertino, California.

"I don't think companies need to be based on a totally new idea."

One concept that business schools try to dispel is that you need a completely original idea to start your own business. Do you believe this?

I think that few companies are started on a totally new idea. Actually I never heard anyone who tried to say that because it is sort of ludicrous. Most companies get started on incremental value-added ideas. What you are trying to do is to give value to the customer.

I would say the fundamental way to start a company is when a new technology allows you to do something fundamentally cheaper than is done in the past, and therefore either broaden the market tremendously—i.e., fax machines—or you take over the existing customer base because it is fundamentally cheaper. So, for example, the minicomputer industry wasn't a brand new idea. It simply allowed us to build computers for the tenth of the price of a mainframe, and now we can apply them into new markets and to new areas and give people the power to do things they couldn't do before.

So I don't think companies need to be based on a totally new idea. What you do have to be able to do is to add value to the customer. We were founded on the idea that the existing software desktop publishing titles were not effectively serving the customer, and we created a product called Q&A which integrated the functions of an existing company's product line called PFS, into a suite. What we did is took three disparate products and integrated them together to improve the functionality.

I was walking around Palo Alto once with Fred Gibbons and Esther Dyson, and we went to a street fair. I went into a bookstore and I said, "Gee Fred, there are no books on PFS." Fred turned to me and said, "I'd fire our documentation people if there ever were a book. Why would you ever need a book? Our products are simple. They have no complexity."

And all of a sudden, the light went on. The fact that people didn't want things that were so low in functionality and so simple was *not* the opportunity. Customers wanted things they could grow into— today's complexity is tomorrow's obvious thing. Customers wanted to adapt the product to their system. I also thought that having books about your product didn't mean the product was deficient, but it just helped build the product's market. While Fred knows more about marketing than I'll ever know, I thought he missed the boat on that issue.

So, it became crystal clear to me that if someone could make a product that did what they did but had richer functionality, people would be able to grow into this product instead of switching to another one. That's where the idea of our company's focus came from—the idea of taking an existing product and adding significant value to the customer through the integration of the products.

So, most companies are not formed on totally new ideas. However, it is absolutely true that you're not going to get rich today by doing what Bill Gates does. One of the things Bill said during a speech, loosely paraphrased, was, "There is no lack of opportunity, but the current opportunity isn't what we've done, because we've already done it. The opportunity is to do something that is new."

These two concepts may seem contradictory, but it depends on your place in the market. Today, in software, an incrementally better spreadsheet has little opportunity. In 1981, an incrementally better spreadsheet had a lot of opportunity. In fact, there have been two incrementally better spreadsheets. VisiCalc, originally invincible, was put out of business by Lotus 1-2-3 which was essentially put out of business by Microsoft Excel. But, at some point, incrementally better just doesn't work.

Thus, the issue really is not whether there is a totally new idea, but whether there is value added to the customer. Is the switching cost of your new product worth its benefit? Is the whole gestalt of your product good enough to convert customers?

When starting a business, I would actually look for areas with some proven track record of need. The highest risk is something that has never been done before, because more often than not, "never done before" means "people don't want it." And, "never done before" usually isn't true—rather, it's usually "never succeeded before."

And, "never succeeded before" could result from bad execution rather than a bad idea. Many people give Phillipe Kahn [founder and former CEO of Borland] credit for Turbo Pascal as if he invented the idea of a low-cost programming package. Not so. There was a Pascal program before Turbo Pascal at the same price point, but it was such a terrible product that it failed. Kahn just had a really good product. The point I'm trying to make is that you must have something that is really worthwhile to the customer, whoever that might be.

How do you determine what is worthwhile to the customer?

Well, the customer decides what is worthwhile to the customer. Customers decide and once they decide it is very difficult to move them.

So is picking the next winning product solely a crapshoot?

No. I think you can do research, you can use intuition, you can spend time with customers—it isn't a crapshoot at all. But successful products serve customers' needs. And if you're trying to replace existing products, then your new product must in some way be of incremental value. Whatever the reason, there must be some value to the customer that is really there.

Customers are smart—start with that. We tried to build our company on the fact that customers are actually intelligent, and mostly make reasonable decisions, and sort out the bullshit from the reality.

In the end, you have to be giving them something of value. It's clear that you can't sell novelty for an extended period of time. Find a pet rock nowadays. There was a time when you couldn't go anywhere without seeing a pet rock. You probably can't buy one today.

What about the idea that customers don't know what they want—the idea that you just create something customers didn't have in mind, but once they see it, they'll purchase it?

Everything is a continuum. No matter what issue we talk about, there are extreme conditions. In math, you focus a lot on boundary conditions. People have a tendency to deal with boundary conditions. The idea that customers don't know what they want is such an example.

The truth is that if you are going to start a business, the best probability of success is in building something that the customers want. It's great to talk about how Procter & Gamble invented mouthwash, and how they came up with this word *halitosis*, and how the early campaigns dealt with convincing people they had a problem and that their mouthwash was the solution. That's great.

Most of the time though, the opportunity isn't in something that customers have no idea about. There is an adage in marketing: you either convince the consumer that he has the disease and then give him the cure, or you sell him the cure because he knows he has the disease. I think you're much better off focusing on businesses where customers know they have the problem, and you give them the cure. It's less risk. Because, in the first case, you must really be sure that you can convince them they have the disease and you have the cure. In Silicon Valley many businesses have tried that approach, and have found out that people didn't really have the disease and thus didn't need the cure.

One of our board members repeatedly says, "Make what you can sell, don't sell what you can make."

Why did you decide to start out on your own? Was it just to create value for the customer? Why not just stay at Digital Research?

Because Digital Research was going to fail. They had incompetent management that couldn't fix the company. They didn't have the will to win. But that's another story. My whole background was in this area. I had started a company before. The opportunities were overwhelming for people with the ability to program and create a product. I said, "Why not?" It seemed like I was at the right place at the right time. There is a lot of luck involved. If people have the willingness and the drive to succeed, then there is a lot of opportunity out there today, especially in software.

But you must have the personality for it. Some people want to be part of a team and don't want to make the decisions. I like to make the decisions. I was watching this football game Monday night. Miami was playing, and they were on the goalline, and it was clear that the coach called in a play. The quarterback sent the other player back to the sidelines and the commentator said, "Well, obviously the quarterback wants to call his own play." I didn't even think they had that option in football, but I thought to myself, "Yeah! There's someone who wants to be in charge."

Not everyone will do that. In order to start a company you have to be willing to take charge and like it. I like the uncertainty of not being able to look to someone else and say, "Gee, what do you think I should do?" When you're in a startup, that's the way it is. You don't have the whole momentum and infrastructure to guide you. You have to make decisions—what to do, who to approach, who to hire. Some people don't feel comfortable doing that. It isn't necessarily bad, it's just different. Different people love different things. And to start a company, you must be able to work in very unclear situations. Take Scott Cook [founder and Chairman of Intuit], for example. Intuit almost failed a number of times. I knew Scott when he first started. He had a vision, and he stuck with that vision. Even in the midst of all that uncertainty, you have to be able to stick with it.

With Symantec, there were many times when we didn't know if we would make the payroll. I remember a time when we gave out stock instead of salary—I still have the certificates which we eventually converted. The point is that you have to be willing to do these types of things—that's one aspect. The other aspect is that you must have an idea that adds value to the customer. And the third thing is you've got to get momentum. Software is a growth and market share business. Nothing else matters.

Software is an 80 percent gross margin business. It's difficult to put a software company out of business. You can't kill it. It's like the monsters in the movies. There aren't enough stakes and garlic in the world to put a software company out of business because the embers keep going—their capital requirements are small. What matters in the software industry is momentum, which is translated into market share and revenue growth.

What makes a company successful from a big-picture point of view is people, process, product, and passion. Concerning people and products: you must have great people and you must have great products. Everyone believes in passion. But as you begin to build a company, you have to balance passion with process or the company will implode.

What do you mean by process?

I mean the systems that enable a company to function as it gets bigger. It's like building a house versus a five-story building—you need different foundations. If you're trying to build a 100-story building, you don't make the decision on how to build a foundation when you're on the third floor. You have to be thinking early on as to what kind of foundation you want to build.

Scale is another way to say this. Having systems that scale is really important in building a company. The systems that scale a large company are its processes. And one of the important processes is hiring great people.

Can you give us an example of process at Symantec?

Early on, when there were only 15 people in this building, everyone was on e-mail. People asked, "Why are we doing this?" We just built e-mail into the culture of the company. Now e-mail is critical to us. We used e-mail long before it was "in." Then, as the company grew, it scaled. The communications system scaled to accommodate more employees.

If you only have passion, it destroys. Look at what happened with Apple. The passion was there, but there wasn't enough process. No one at the time could figure out that the Apple II was pretty important and was paying all the bills. In retrospect, it was pretty obvious.

Consider the internet. You can't have a logical discussion about the internet nowadays. You just can't. In a year or two, some of these companies will crash and burn, except for those that have the value-added to the customer. Everyone will say, "Oh yeah, it was obvious." But right now you cannot have a rational discussion about it. Passion overwhelms in the short term.

Another important process early on is to get really good people who can last for a period of time. We have a really good CFO named Bob Dykes. He's been with us for years. When we hired him, we weren't looking for a great CFO of a $50 million company; we were looking for a CFO of a billion dollar company. And we wanted someone who was willing to see us through to that. That's the difference.

I often hear venture capitalists say that they want to find a really good startup company marketing person. I don't know what that means. What you want is someone who will be a good senior manager of a billion dollar company. If that is not your vision, you don't belong in the Valley. Building well—that is what it's about. For that you need people who can manage growth along the way. The worst thing is to have a company where you continually bring in new people over the existing people, because the existing ones can't grow, or the company is "expanding." There are always nice ways of saying it. That's what drives me crazy.

It's better to start with really good people and then build under them. Even with our relatively small size, promoting from within is almost iron-clad. We won't hire anybody at a senior level from the outside. Take college recruiting. Our policy is to hire people from school and promote from within. These are examples of processes that you must put in place in a nascent company.

How do you find the right people?

You must not only find really smart people but those who want to be part of a company that scales from five to a thousand employees. And you must find people who have seen it. Often these are tough people to manage. On paper, we shouldn't have hired Bob Dykes because he is strong-willed and he can be tough to manage, but you must hire enough people who can envision how the company might be run.

The typical startup story is of a couple of guys who create a computer company in their garage. But Apple, for example, wouldn't have gone anywhere without guys like Markkula [A. C. "Mike" Markkula, the former Chairman and President of Apple, and one of Apple's earliest employees/investors], who had some idea of what a company looked like and knew about things like human resources and finance. In general, you can't just wing it. Now, the founder doesn't have to have that experience, but he better be willing to go out and get the experience.

You mentioned the need for people who can make the business grow. How do you keep good ideas bubbling up within the company?

We have product groups and teams that work together that have a lot of autonomy so long as their market share grows. Within those product groups, they can create products which lead us in new directions. Today, if you're a general manager, you give me a plan and I'll give you a compensation package that lets you triple your base salary if you can exceed your revenue plan by a specified amount. As long as you deliver 100 percent of the revenue and 100 percent of the operating profits you have wide latitude in how you go about doing it.

One of the common refrains regarding starting one's own business is, "I would start a business if I had the money..." In C & E's case, you had already made your money from the sale of a previous company.

If someone said something like that to me, my answer would be, "Yeah, if I gave you a lot of money to spend, you could spend the money." Big deal. It doesn't take great talent to spend money. If everything were free, I'd have a lot more. It's like the *Twilight Zone* episode where the guy dies and he goes to heaven and everything is perfect: he is playing pool and shoots the cue ball and all the colored balls go in and nothing ever goes wrong. He finally gets very frustrated and says to himself, "I'm in heaven and it's driving me crazy." The punchline, of course, is that he made the wrong assumption—he wasn't in heaven at all!

The money's there if you have a good idea. It all goes back to your product. I think it's sort of a cop-out to say, "I couldn't get the money." It's hard to raise money, I admit. I knocked on a lot of doors and got turned down by almost everyone. It's good though, because when I see them, I point out how much money I've made. But, the people who did invest made serious amounts of money. We were a real home run for people like Kleiner [Kleiner, Perkins, Caufield & Byers, a venture capital firm]. But we were a long shot—I guess they all are.

You must recognize that the issue is getting and selling the idea. If you have the right idea and can sell it you will eventually get your opportunity. And software was the best business because capital requirements were so low.

I was turned down by virtually everyone except the Masters Fund in Denver. Only one person funded C & E initially. And then Kleiner got involved because they wanted us to acquire Symantec because Symantec was going out of business. So we took it over basically and got more funding from Kleiner. I talked to everyone in the Valley. I literally bought a condo at Sand Hill Circle [Sand Hill Road in Menlo Park is the largest concentration of venture capital firms in the world]. In that regard, I had money. Maybe the difference was that I could afford to take the time; I didn't need a job.

But I still would have started my own company. And, I don't know of too many people who would have been successful had they had the money when starting out. Some people just don't want to be entrepreneurs. It's a very unstructured, hazy process with a lot of uncertainty, and you're the one making all the decisions. Every morning you decide whether to knock on Kleiner's door or Mayfield's. What's the answer? You have to be turned down many times before you succeed.

It's hard to say that in the U.S. and Silicon Valley good ideas go in want for funding. Let's get real. This is a society where entrepreneurs are welcomed, encouraged, and have every opportunity. There is a great group of proven people here willing to help entrepreneurs become successful.

Another piece of advice for raising money is to go with the best [venture capitalists], and give them more equity. I'll take a worse deal from Kleiner any day of the week. They have people like John Doerr. You can't put into words what that makes. I've heard people say to me, "I'm looking at these three companies as potential partners and I'm going to go with this one because I give up less." This is totally brain-dead thinking. You're looking at linear differences when victory is exponential returns. What you want to do is to turn linear growth into exponential growth. I always say having John Doerr and the best people are best for good reason: their track record in making average opportunities successful ones is infinitely higher than the second-tier venture capitalists.

Money is available in Silicon Valley. I have no sympathy for people whining that they can't get money. When you do get money, go to the best.

You've talked a lot about great people and great employees. How does your acquisition strategy fit with your need to have great people? How do you find out if the acquired company has good people?

We look for great products in markets where the company is winning and we assume that they wouldn't be there if they weren't somehow very talented. Within every company there are really great people. If you identify them and give them a chance to succeed it really helps build the company.

There isn't really one Symantec—it's a bunch of people from a bunch of different companies. It's like a melting pot. This is a ridiculous comparison, but Symantec's strength is similar to America's. From many highly motivated people from many different places and different viewpoints came a great country. When we acquire we take the core product team and keep them together.

One of the criticisms of your company is that its product line is just too broad. This keeps you from taking advantage of product synergies. Should you trim your product line?

Most companies, when they get to the half-billion-dollar size, have a pretty broad product line. We do software for desktop computers and the networks they are attached to. That's all we do. It's very synergistic.

We've really had a hard time shaking the image of being a conglomerate. And we've been guilty of some of this. We started out with Q&A, then decided to acquire. At some point, it became clear to me that suites and Microsoft in particular would dominate productivity software. They may not have competed with us head-to-head, but we decided to transition to utilities. We made the transition successfully but it turns out that the software utility business is cyclic with operating systems and networks. Then we really looked at utilities, networks, and communications. These are really the three things we are in. There are many synergies and shared technologies in our product line. We don't do lots of other things we could do. We're pretty focused.

Unfortunately, this hurts us on Wall Street. Wall Street rewards pure plays more than anything else because Wall Street understands pure plays. They want to know what's hot, who the pure plays are, and buy. They want to know what's out, who are the pure plays in this segment, and sell.

So will we ever see a Norton game?

Probably not. We certainly wouldn't put the Norton brand name on it. We've done a lot of brand name research. With Norton, the brand is deep but narrow. A lot of people have said, "Just put the Norton name on everything instead of Symantec." This would be a big mistake. I want to be sure to protect the Norton brand name and be very careful with brand extensions of the Norton line. Here you have a real human being, Peter Norton. It's almost better than Betty Crocker.

I wanted to talk about your relationship with Microsoft. Why doesn't Microsoft just put more of your product's functionality into its own products?

They already have.

So, aren't you afraid that you'll be pushed out of the market?

No. Not really. Our business adds value to operating systems. It's the most proven software business in existence. We add value to knowledge users. We have a tremendous infrastructure that works closely with Microsoft. This is a tremendous barrier to competition. In the spreadsheet market there's not much of a barrier, because they all use the same APIs [Application Programming Interfaces] and they're all public. Utilities, however, work deep in the innards of the operating system. It's very complicated stuff and requires tremendous personal relationships between their development teams and ours. This isn't stuff that is legislated by Mike Maples [a senior executive at Microsoft], it happens at the lower levels of the company. They can't have relationships with many different companies. That's the kind of stuff that is a huge barrier to our competition.

Yes, but that doesn't keep Microsoft from incorporating your software's functionality into their own?

No. But, they're not motivated to do this. There's no return on investment for them because they would have to support it for the *whole* market. We focus on a reasonable piece of the market. Take anti-virus functionality as an example: Microsoft put it in DOS 6 but pulled it out of Windows 95. The anti-virus market has taken off now and everyone has benefited.

Doesn't this arrangement give Microsoft a lot of power over Symantec? They could always collaborate with some other company.

I guess in theory, but it's hard to see the motivation for it. And it's hard to cultivate these relationships overnight. The problem with these business cases, that you fellows study in business school when you sit and talk in a circular room, is that a business is *not* like a machine where all the connections are firm and when you toggle one switch the other one toggles just as you would predict.

Organizations actually are very different—when you toggle one thing, something entirely different may happen from what you predicted. Microsoft can't just tell their people, "Forget all these relationships, we're going to screw Symantec." Many people would think it very unfair, and we'd know about it before most of their management knew.

Microsoft is not this evil empire, as many would have you believe. They're actually very solid business people. That's why we work with Microsoft. Apple, on the other hand, has a problem. It's as if every week there's a new strategy and some new intrigue going on. Life is just too short to put up with this bullshit. Microsoft runs a solid business. They're honest. You can trust them. You can believe what they tell you.

This isn't common conventional wisdom now.

Well, it's the truth.

What about Microsoft's closed system software?

Every system's closed. Everyone has their own advantage.

Well, what about UNIX?

UNIX is closed and dispersed. There are just various different closed versions even though people talk collectively about an open UNIX. What bothers me most about the industry today is that people spend more time thinking about how to do Microsoft in than about how to help customers. If people just focused on doing good things for customers, things would take care of themselves.

Microsoft's day will come. I mean, no one is invincible. In a business where technology races so quickly, it's funny how people spend so much time on Microsoft. Microsoft isn't like the Robber Barons who had an impenetrable iron grip on the infrastructure. The Robber Barons had economies of scale with their factories and right-of-way with railroads. There was no way to compete with them.

This is *so* different. I think that monopolies are actually really good in this environment because the monopoly serves the customer by providing standards, and the pace of technology eventually does the monopoly in, and creates a stability of plateaus.

Plateaus?

For example, IBM was invincible with mainframes. They missed the minicomputer. DEC and Data General raced in and created invincible monopolies which were subsequently done in by the PC.

I think that there is too much focus on Microsoft. Every time the industry tries to do them in, they do themselves in. Instead of focusing on them, let's really focus on something that customers want. That's a much better model.

Many say that an entrepreneur's success mainly amounts to luck, and that there are so many people in the Valley that are talented, but only a select few like yourselves are CEOs—

First of all, I don't think that you can presuppose that being the CEO is the ultimate thing—

You don't think it is?

Well, *I* like the job but not everyone might. Do you think Jerry Rice wishes he were quarterback? Do you think Steve Young wishes he were a wide receiver? Great people can do different things.

Second, chance is the dominant force in life, within bands.

Within bands?

Talented people do well. But how well they do is really up to chance.

Is Bill Gates *really* that much smarter? I doubt he thinks that. But he worked his ass off. He was driven, focused, had a take-no-prisoners attitude, was competitive, paranoid, and didn't take no for an answer—all the traits of success. But for everyone who runs a company there are hundreds of people with equal talent and ability that weren't in the right place at the right time.

I was a submarine officer in the Navy. They sent me to get a master's degree in computer science. I thought that postgraduate school was a ticket-punch. But, I wanted some excitement, so I chose a hard thesis advisor—Gary Kildall—who was into microcomputers, and here we are.

Gary might not have been in his office the day I knocked on his door, or he could have told me he didn't want any more thesis students—all kinds of things could have happened. To believe that you have some predestiny is very naïve. But, on the other hand, I think that of the people who are given equal opportunities, some people do better than others.

So, luck is important, but at the same time, I think that understanding the common threads between the CEOs—being able to work in a world of uncertainty and being able to make decisions without perfect information—is crucial. It's like in the Navy—the most exciting aspect was that you're driving the submarine around, you're the officer of the deck, and you're making the decisions in a world where there isn't a perfect answer. And, I think that, in some ways, business is the same thing. You have an end objective, but there isn't a lot of guidance on how to get there. I like that.

4

STEVE CASE

America Online

IT'S THE CUSTOMER, STUPID.

Steve Case used to be a shampoo salesman. He didn't sell door-to-door, but he did develop marketing strategies for shampoo and toothpaste while at Procter & Gamble. Case graduated from Williams College with a liberal arts degree and, at age 37, is one of *Giants'* youngest CEOs. Like Scott Cook (who also worked at P&G before founding Intuit), Case strongly believed in an idea for a product, and persisted with his belief until the idea succeeded. With Cook, the idea was financial services software. In the case of Case, the idea was online interactive services.

What are online interactive services? Anyone who ever has surfed the internet or used America Online (AOL) knows. Interactive services allow a user to transmit and manipulate valuable information—or "content"—to a user sitting at a computer. For example, AOL customers can download stock quotes, book airline tickets, read popular magazines such as *Newsweek* and *Time*, or even chat with other AOL customers about the next episode of *Oprah*. The service is "interactive" because the user requests and manipulates specific data for his or her own use.

Providing content has become big business. The number of companies offering content on the internet is exploding exponentially. So how does AOL differ from the internet? Case is happy to explain. First, AOL is much simpler to use. AOL's interface allows a user to easily log on and navigate to easily located content that is selected and placed (i.e., packaged) by AOL employees. Second, AOL spends millions on direct mail and advertising to build brand recognition. All of those floppy disks in the mail you get are a small part of their huge campaign.

This marketing strategy has proven to be powerfully effective. AOL has become the largest number one commercial online service provider in the world, with millions of subscribers. Located in Vienna, Virginia, the company has over 5,000 employees worldwide, and had over $350 million in revenues in 1995.

Yet AOL's story is not one of overnight success. The company was co-founded in 1985 by Case and struggled for a long time. AOL's turning point came when Case partnered with PC manufacturers by bundling his online service with their computers in the hope that consumers would log on. They did, and AOL began to flourish.

Today, AOL is expanding its base overseas with online services such as AOL Germany, and other international providers. But, with only 10 percent of households in the United States using online services, Case feels there is plenty of room for AOL to grow at home.

We met with Steve Case at AOL's new headquarters in Reston, Virginia.

"Technology-based markets just take a while before they hit their stride."

Tell us about the startup process and what it was like. Ten years later, what are the most vivid incidents in your mind?

AOL was founded in 1985, but I actually became interested in online services in the late 1970s. In 1983, I joined a company in Virginia that had essentially an online video game. And in 1983, Atari video games were the rage—not many consumers had PCs at the time.

The notion was that you would plug a modem into the game machine and turn it into an interactive terminal. I thought that was a terrific idea, so I joined the company. It was a terrific idea, but the timing turned out to be horrible because our new video game product was coming to market just when the Atari video game market crashed—so the company was not going to work.

But, some of the people I met during my work there ended up being the co-founders of what became America Online in 1985. We were able to attract a modest amount of venture capital, about a million dollars.

In 1985, the biggest deal we did at the time was a distribution and marketing agreement with Commodore. The Commodore 64 was the dominant home computer back then, and we thought we could eliminate a lot of the market risk and expense of launching this new company if we had a marketing partner like Commodore. We structured a deal where Commodore agreed to bundle our service with all of their Commodore 64 computers and all of their Commodore modems. We broke even our second year in business with 50,000 Commodore customers and figured that we'd do it again.

So, we then went to Apple, and convinced them to do essentially the same deal. And then we went to Tandy and asked, "Don't you want to join us too?" They agreed. So the first five years of the company's existence were spent partnering with PC manufacturers—first Commodore, then Apple, then Tandy, then IBM. We essentially created private-label online services for each brand of computer by leveraging their marketing distribution clout to generate awareness.

It was only about five years ago that the company came into its own and had a critical mass of people and technology to kind of fend for ourselves. That's when we launched America Online as our own brand and started aggregating these separate brands together under America Online. So it was a fairly gradual process and a typical bootstrap. We had a little bit of capital and a big idea and succeeded by targeting each segment of the market and partnering with PC manufacturers to reduce a lot of the financial requirements and marketing risks.

It's hard to argue with your success today—you have 6 million customers—but for several years, you didn't grow that quickly. What pitfalls could you have avoided?

Most of the slow growth had to do with market timing. A lot of these technology-based markets just take a while—usually a decade—before they hit their stride. For most of the interesting technologies, like graphical user interfaces or multimedia, it takes about a decade for them to come together.

We would have grown slowly in those first few years no matter what. The other thing that really inhibited our ability to grow was capital constraints. We were a little company with a few dozen people, with some money in the bank, but not a lot.

When we started in 1985, we were competing with big companies that had lots of money—particularly IBM, Sears, and CBS. In retrospect, it [having little capital] was probably the best thing that happened to us, because it forced us to be a little bit nimbler and think more like guerilla marketers and to provide a service that people really liked. We had to use word-of-mouth and figure out clever ways to partner with a wide variety of companies in order to do things more efficiently. Had somebody given us more capital early on, it probably would have been a bad thing.

You wouldn't have been as clever from a marketing perspective?

Right. In some respects, it's similar to when rock stars become famous when they're 18 years old and are unable to handle it as well as when they're 35 years old. It's hard to be an overnight success. We had the luxury of learning as we went along, making a tremendous number of mistakes, and remaining relatively invisible. We had learned a lot of important lessons before we were in the limelight.

And I feel sorry for some of these companies that the whole world is watching, because they really don't have a chance to grow up.

Do you expect this with many of the internet companies that have recently gone public?

Sure, but it's a good news/bad news thing. The good news is that you start a company, a year later it's worth a lot of money, everybody's excited, and the company gets a lot of press.

For some, particularly Netscape, it has turned out terrifically well. They have leveraged that momentum to create a brand, and are now leveraging that brand into the internet business.

But there is bad news too. Many of these startups have perceived success before they have actual success. Some of their concepts are riveting, but generate very little revenue and no profits. And at some point, people ask, "Where's the beef?" And I think it will be more difficult for them. I'm not sure whether it is good or bad. It's just different than our experience bootstrapping and building up over time.

If you graph the number of AOL subscribers over time, it looks like a hockey stick.

Everybody talks about it, but it never actually happens. In our case, it did.

So what happened at the inflection point? What was the critical juncture?

A number of things happened and some of them related to the development of the market. We really hit our stride two or three years ago. Part of it involves having a better product, very strong acceptance, and very strong word-of-mouth—even when we were number 3 to CompuServe and Prodigy. We coupled that with more aggressive marketing and built our infrastructure to handle the demand we were creating.

We also benefited in the last couple of years from sluggish competitors. Prodigy was confused because IBM and Sears argued for several years about investing more or selling off, so there was a lack of direction there. Even CompuServe was saddled by H&R Block ownership. H&R Block thought of it more as a source of earnings and was less willing to aggressively invest in it.

But, the center of it all is having a better product. In the subscription business, all we can do, in terms of marketing, is to get people to try the service. One thing I learned at Procter & Gamble is that bright marketing just kills a bad product faster. You can't force a customer to pay you money every month, but you can encourage anybody to try anything once, particularly if it's free. That was our trial strategy.

Customers won't pay you money every month for many years if they don't like your offering. So it's got to be a great service, one that captivates you. Anything else is secondary.

Who are your major competitors? A couple of years ago you talked about Microsoft. Now some consider AT&T as your biggest threat in this market.

It's hard to say. What's interesting, if you look back at the last ten years, is that most of our presumptive competitors have stumbled. Every year in the past ten, there has been somebody who was supposedly going to enter and dominate the market, and every year it changes.

Three years ago, for example, the conventional wisdom was that interactive TV was going to be the real business while online services were just a transitional business; therefore, TCI and friends would really drive interactive TV. Two years ago, the dominant notion was that the media companies would try this. Time Warner was launching Pathfinder, Rupert Murdoch bought Delphi, and there was a flurry of activity in the media companies.

A year ago, Microsoft was going to dominate the market.

Today the conventional wisdom is that telephone companies will dominate the market, because they will provide low-priced internet access like AT&T, or Pacific Bell, or cable companies. But these things just don't pan out like they are supposed to. Part of the reason for this is that big companies can focus too much on a big press release and not enough on creating a product or service that millions of consumers can fall in love with. They think it's their God-given right to have a chunk of the market because of who they are. Companies must earn it through execution. Nobody anoints you a player in this market. So, today, I think it is difficult to predict who our competitors will be in the next few years. And, some of the companies that are perceived to be competitors may actually turn out to be partners, such as AT&T.

If anybody is going to compete with us, they are going to have to reach out to the mainstream computer audience with an experience that's easier to use and/or more useful and/or more fun and/or more affordable. And if they don't do that they won't be competitive, irrespective of what brand they bring or how much money they throw into it. Prodigy has proved that throwing money at a problem doesn't give you a lock on business. In the last decade, a lot of major companies and major brands have entered and exited this business.

How have you been able to stave off your competitors?

We've always had a clear view of what this was all about. We've always focused, for example, heavily on the consumer market, whereas some of our competitors dillydally between business and consumers.

We've always said that in consumer marketing you must create a service that is easy to use, useful, fun, and affordable and if consumers fall in love with it—you'll do well, and if they don't—you won't. Everything else is peripheral to that core idea of creating a more compelling consumer experience that people can't get anywhere else.

It must excite them so much that they'll run down the street and tell their neighbors and their relatives to get online too. That's really the core of what we are about, and even though there are many tactical or opportunistic strategies we can take in terms of alliances and the like, they are all a means to an end. In the end, we will create a mainstream market for tens of millions of people, with AOL as the preeminent brand.

Since only one-third of Americans use PCs, do you think you'll shift to a different medium anytime soon?

We don't care about the delivery system. AOL is about interactive experience that can excite the imagination of tens of millions of consumers. We don't much care whether it's delivered through PCs or PDAs [personal digital assistants, i.e., Apple's Newton] or settop boxes on TVs. As technology becomes more mainstream, you'll have simpler, more affordable access devices. I'm sure that will happen. There are some signs of that happening now.

One hundred years ago people were saying, "I don't see why anyone would want a telephone." It actually took several decades before the adoption curve rose. The same thing happened with fax machines in the late '70s and early '80s. Now interactive services are experiencing the same evolution pattern.

We believe that the majority of people will use these services because online interactive services can fundamentally enhance people's lives. Back in 1985, we were alone with the view that the killer applications for consumers were going to be interactive services. We felt that not that many people used typewriters. Very few consumers needed a database, but everybody buys products and services and everybody is interested in meeting other people, and everybody is interested in being informed or watching television.

Those are the things that can be done more effectively through interactive services. So, it may take a while, but it will be mainstream. We've been at this for more than a decade, and we'll be at it for a lot longer. We're still pretty young.

In the future, do you foresee developing applications? In that sense, will we see AOL word processors and spreadsheets and the like?

Not really. It depends on what you mean by that. We do believe that, if we do our job right, more consumers will use AOL in a more official way. We want AOL to be their primary dashboard, not just in the world of services, but in other things, so in that sense we do want to enhance the functionality within the AOL environment as much as possible. For example, our view is that for people who are interested in paying bills it would be better to have a bill-paying application sitting within AOL, instead of having to close AOL and load Quicken.

At the same time, I don't see any particular value in an AOL spreadsheet. We have spreadsheet and graphic technology built into AOL but it's concentric. For example, if you go into our personal finance area and you look at a stock's historical quotes, you can instantly have that graphed. Essentially, that graphic function is built into AOL in order to bring content to life.

Of the executives that we are interviewing, you and Scott Cook are the only ones without backgrounds in technology. Has this been a hindrance to you?

I don't consider it a hindrance. It may even be helpful because—and Scott Cook [the founder of Intuit, developer of Quicken] is similar in that both of us worked at Procter & Gamble—we're both essentially trying to build mainstream consumer services. To steal from the Clinton campaign a few years ago: It's the consumer, stupid. That's all that matters and everything else is a means to an end.

So, there was never a point when you thought, "Maybe if I had better understood this emerging technology, the company might have been more successful."

I don't think so. We have extraordinarily bright people here, so we are not often surprised. We usually have the ability to see around the corners—that's one of the benefits of being a market leader. You tend to be a magnet for ideas and people that come knocking on your door as opposed to being surprised when they're formally introduced.

You started AOL at a pretty early age. What are your weaknesses as a manager, entrepreneur, and CEO, and how do you compensate?

The main one is focusing more on getting to the promised land and less on the steps that need to be taken to get there. The details of running a big company do not excite me. But it's part of the game you have to play. What excites me is the opportunity to reach out and touch the lives of tens of millions of consumers and establish AOL as the preeminent brand. I just don't find many of the day-to-day activities all that riveting.

The other related weakness is impatience. I want stuff to happen *now*. I don't want to have an endless meeting to talk about things, or a task force to consider them. I want action *now*, and, in general, that's appropriate. But in some cases, structure is helpful—particularly if things are changing rapidly and you have 5,000 employees and you need to make sure a clear message is being articulated.

These things are easy to balance by bringing in a world-class executive team. It really is a balancing act, and we've done that quite successfully in the past few years. Our most effective recruitment strategy in terms of executive talent has been acquiring companies led by terrific CEOs who then play strong leadership roles within the company.

Let's talk a little bit about AOL's social responsibility. I have a teenage cousin who logged on to AOL and was able to access some of the chat rooms that contained adult material. How do you handle that?

Our approach has been to err on the side of diversity and freedom of expression, while empowering each of our members—especially parents—to customize and control the experience for their households. For example, we have parental controls on AOL so parents can decide what parts of AOL and/or the internet they do or don't want their kids to see. They can actually customize this for each child. So, if parents want to block access to all chat rooms or some chat rooms or all web sites or some web sites they have the capability to do that.

We don't feel that our role in life is to play God and decide what is or isn't appropriate for different families or different communities or even different countries. We have to recognize that one of the more important attributes of this new medium is that it is interactive and participatory and everyone can participate as opposed to traditional media where a small group of editors or producers basically decided what everybody read and watched.

But we don't believe that the anything-goes, wild-west atmosphere is appropriate either.

The problem with parental controls is that many of your users are kids, and often, they understand the technology a lot better than their parents do.

I think that's fair. But, I think the parents should have the responsibility of what happens in their household. It's tragic if parents abdicate their responsibility to the school or the government or to a business like AOL. Parents have to be responsible for the upbringing of their kids, because every parent has different guidelines for what they think is appropriate. The only alternative for that is to have broad-based government censorship—other countries have it—where the government decides what you should or shouldn't see, and that's foolhardy.

In society, people have choices. There are laws that people are expected to abide by, and if they don't there is some punishment associated with it. We have some guidelines at AOL for our members. If people do anything we don't think is appropriate, we take action, including throwing them off AOL. But, we do believe that the primary responsibility must be with our members, particularly the responsibility for how kids access interactive services. We're not going to become the latch-key parents for tens of millions of kids around the country. That's not something we are particularly suited to do and it is inappropriate for us to do.

Okay. How about your responsibilities as a manager and as a parent? Balancing work and family life issues is a pretty big topic these days. How do you do it?

With some difficulty. But I don't believe the issue is to do all of one thing or all of another. The way I do it is partly by recognizing that I have some control of time and space. Much of what I do, I can do anywhere. I don't have to physically be here a lot. A lot of what I have to do is done by the telephone. For example, next week I'm going to take my kids to Hawaii, where I was born and raised, and we will be there for about ten days. What I typically do is get up in the morning before they get up and spend an hour or two in the office, make a phone call or two and read some e-mail.

So how many hours on average do you work per week?

I don't really count it that way because the work is always there. It's not like I'm going to Tahiti and will be completely disconnected from the world. If something is breaking, I'll focus on it. If not, I won't.

Twenty, forty, eighty?

Hours are nothing. Sixty to eighty range.

Has your work ethic changed over the history of the company?

No, not really. That's more a function of still being passionate about what you are doing. I'm sure that if someday I get bored without new challenges, then it would be different. I'm doing this because I want to, not because I have to.

Where do you think are the next new opportunities in technology?

The big wave will be providing the fuel to drive interactive services into the mainstream market. That's going to be as important over the next decade as software was for the last decade. In the long run, people who are building original, unique content that leverages this medium in building new brands are going to do well.

But thinking that content is king is naïve. It's only going to be king if it's truly original and linked to leveraged distribution. The barriers to entry for content creation today are very low, because anybody can create a website and get a big distribution list. And that means there will be millions of websites.

Consumers don't want millions of websites. They don't want to click on "Sports" and have 18 thousand sports websites pop up. That's not the way consumers will use these services. They will rely on people to package and present the services that are going to be of the highest quality and the most relevant to their particular interest—so being plugged into a dashboard is going to be important to distribution—an aspect that I think is underestimated. That will be the big lesson in the next couple of years.

What kind of advice would you give people who are trying to startup their own interactive service companies?

Probably the most significant one is to do something you really love, are really passionate about, and that matters to you. Take a long-term view and be really patient. There *are* going to be bumps in the road— there always are—and in this particular market there will probably be more because the set of expectations that have been created won't be met.

If you take a long-term view, like the parable of the tortoise and the hare, you have a good chance of being there at the finish line. But, if you get caught up in the heat of it and are just looking for the quick hit, whether it be the quick IPO or a quick deal, you'll hit the wall.

5

SCOTT COOK

Intuit

IT'S THE CUSTOMER, STUPID. PART II

Scott Cook's preparation for life as a computer software founder and chairman was to work in product marketing at Procter & Gamble. Don't laugh—both Cook and America Online chief Steve Case credit their P&G heritage for giving them the marketing savvy necessary to create leading consumer software products in a rapidly shifting market.

Cook's company, Intuit, is best known for its popular Quicken line of personal finance software. The company has also expanded to provide tax preparation software (TurboTax) and has made a huge entry into the online banking business.

In the ten years since its founding, Intuit boasts yearly revenues in excess of $500M and is perhaps the only company that can claim to have competed head-to-head against mighty Microsoft—and won.

Cook's idea for a new software product came while sitting at his dining room table, and subsequent success is the stuff entrepreneurial dreams are made of. One evening, while seeing his wife pay bills, Cook concluded that what the world could really use was a practical, "intuitive" software application that magically ordered the tangled rat's nest of one's checking and savings accounts. Inspired, he promptly drew up a business plan and wandered over to Stanford's engineering department in order to post a notice for students interested in doing some programming for a startup company. Tom Proulx, a computer science student lounging in a courtyard, asked to look at Cook's notice. A partnership was born.

Securing funding for the company wasn't as easy. Cook was shown in—and out—of the offices of dozens of venture capital firms without a single offer of interest. But in a supreme vote of confidence, Cook's family and friends emptied their savings accounts to fund his young venture.

The investment proved to be a wise one as Intuit's product eventually gained market acceptance and has dominated the market ever since, with over 12 million people using Quicken. Intuit's culture of a strong customer focus is rooted in Cook's marketing background and sets the company apart from most other technology-focused software companies.

Subsequent to Bill Gates' decision to acquire its pesky competitor, Intuit became a household name. It also led to a reinvigorated effort by the Department of Justice to control Microsoft for monopolistic size and practices. The specter of an ax-wielding DOJ proved too threatening to Gates, who scuttled the deal with Cook—an initial disappointment that he now claims was best for Intuit.

Intuit is now focused on extending its hegemony into online banking. It has already made a number of deals with financial institutions around the world and promises to solve the financial headaches of many customers plagued by mysterious black holes in their checking and savings accounts.

Intuit's headquarters are located in Mountain View, California. We conducted our interview on an outdoor bench in the heart of the Intuit Campus.

"The scary thing about entrepreneurial companies is that they grow up to be reflections of their founders."

Let's talk about the early days at Intuit. Legend has it that you approached, and were turned down, by over thirty venture capital firms for funding.

It was twenty-something.

Why was it so difficult? It seems that you had good credentials.

We thought it would be an easy, fun decision for the venture capitalists to fund us because we had done a lot of market research and had really studied the customer. We understood the problems with the existing competing products on the market and had already built our own product. With a well-researched business plan and a working product, we thought it would be easy to get money.

Boy, were we wrong. One hundred and eighty degrees wrong. We couldn't even get second meetings with most of the VCs. One reason is that our management team had no industry experience. I was a former fat salesman [Cook marketed Crisco while at P&G] and my partner Tom [Proulx] was still a student. Another reason is that the investors fundamentally didn't believe in the business. In fact, there were occasional newspaper and magazine articles that recommended against buying computers for managing checkbooks and recipes. Another reason is that ours was a consumer product and most VC investing at the time was in industrial products. Investors were not comfortable with a business as different as consumer products, which is reasonable; you shouldn't invest in things you're not comfortable with. I also think there was a fundamental disbelief that a market existed for computers in the home. Those four reasons are probably enough to sink most good ideas.

Did you ever start to believe that what they were saying was right?

No. We had the data and had studied the customer. We knew we were building what customers wanted. We just couldn't figure out how to get them to buy it since we were supposedly going to use the venture capital money to solve that. It was a real problem.

The key to business success is knowing your customer cold. We had spent time understanding the customer. We clearly understood customer behavior and had data showing that our solution was vastly better according to customers' decision-making criteria. Our big fear was that, without money, our competitors would see what we were doing and recognize that ours was a superior product and copy it. Had any competitor lifted its pinky to compete with us, we would have been history. We were so weak for so long. The competition had retail presence, momentum, money, and brand names. We had none of that.

Wasn't it your father who lent you money from his retirement savings?

It's a real story of entrepreneurship. Very few entrepreneurs in this country are backed by venture capitalists, perhaps one percent. The other ninety-nine percent could never have gotten venture capital for their business. I used retirement savings from my job, my dad loaned me money, my mom loaned me money, and I used lines of credit. Also, banks invented a great thing called *line of credit*—they don't ask what the money is for.

We often worked without money. We started paying salaries and then had to stop. At the suggestion of someone in the company, we tried getting a few people who knew us to invest smaller amounts of money. We got his father-in-law and a former boss to invest. We had asked for $2 million from VCs and we received $151,000 from these smaller investors—much less than what we were looking for. It represented a total change to the business plan, but it kept the doors open for another six months. Without that investment we wouldn't be here today.

What advice would you give to entrepreneurs looking for financing?

Financing is really not the most important issue. If you have a great business, know your customer, and know that what you are doing is superior to what's on the market—that's what it takes to win. But if you have a lousy business idea, financing won't turn it into a good one. Getting money is a necessary requirement, but I really wouldn't focus on the financing. I would focus on knowing the customer cold.

In the case of products like Quicken, how do you do great market research?

It depends on the question you are asking.

We needed to understand the financial habits and attitudes of households. The only way to find that information out was to talk to households. So I'd make calls and I got my sister-in-law to call households. We asked upper-income consumers—they were the only people buying computers—about their financial lives. We did this to build a real gut knowledge about how real people did their finances: their behaviors, their likes, and their dislikes. We looked at behavioral data as well. It became very clear to us that people wanted a way to take the hassle out of doing their finances. Who likes to pay bills and write in checkbooks?

The key here is that great business breakthroughs occur at the intersection of what customers really want and what technology does well. True greatness is in that intersection. There are many things out there that technology does well but customers don't want. Conversely, I know I could sell shoes that make you fly, but I can't quite get the technology to work.

What do I mean by what people want? People won't tell you what they want. If they simply said they wanted X, you wouldn't need a marketing department. Often they can't verbalize what they want because they typically don't understand things they haven't seen much of. They will give you an answer, but it may not be the right answer. You must understand their fundamental motivations and attitudes. My answer is to use several techniques. Behavioral data is useful. That's why you have usability labs. We used these to understand customers' actual behaviors and found that the data completely supported our thinking that the existing products had completely missed the mark in terms of delivering what people wanted.

The amazing thing is that companies—particularly technology-based companies—often miss what customers really want because they focus on their technology.

Gordon Eubanks (of Symantec) recalled an old marketing adage: you can either convince a customer he has a disease and sell him your cure, or you can sell your cure for a disease he already knows he has.

They can't verbalize what they want, particularly when it comes to new stuff. If you're talking about a new kind of product, customers will do a lousy job of verbalizing when directly asked what they want. To find the answer you must go to the fundamentals of their habits and practices.

For example, in the1920s nobody said that they wanted radio entertainment. People couldn't imagine that sort of thing. In

Pittsburgh, a group of entrepreneurs focused on this new radio technology. At the time, the technology hadn't achieved significant usage because technologists focused on the technology instead of understanding what customers wanted. This group of entrepreneurs in Pittsburgh reasoned that, if they sold everybody half a radio—just the receiver, not a transformer—and if they transmitted just one way— not two ways, as everyone was thinking—and if they broadcasted entertainment, and if they paid for it with commercials so that the entertainment was free to the listener—then, wow—a lot of people would want that.

That's the kind of commercial innovation that causes technology to really explode and change our lives. Had those entrepreneurs walked around surveying people and asking them if they wanted to listen to music on the radio, people would have said no. But if you understand that people fundamentally like entertainment, especially if delivered for free, you have the opportunity to address a key set of fundamentals.

Technologists often use the Macintosh as an example of how true innovation doesn't require customer feedback.

There was tremendous customer feedback with Macintosh. Anyone could see that then-existing computers were a bitch to use. As a consumer problem, it hit you in the face. And it was so obvious that they didn't need to talk to consumers to notice that they found computers difficult to use. Any idiot could tell you they were difficult!

But you can't hold up the Mac as a great example of fundamental invention because it leveraged so much stuff from Xerox PARC. Instead, it's a great example of commercial innovation—figuring out how to package technology and make it a commercial success. Xerox had everything, but they couldn't make it a commercial success.

But the essence of your earlier assertion, the importance of customer analysis, focus groups, and feedback, was not a part of the Macintosh.

And it almost killed them. It got them going, but they couldn't build a volume market. The corporate marketplace asked for several changes to the product architecture. And frankly, that tradition of Apple not listening to customers has bedeviled the company for a decade. In

Microsoft, you see a company that's constantly listening to, learning from, and implementing customer feedback. It's one of the reasons why Microsoft has outstripped Apple's success at Apple's own game.

I've worked with both Apple and Microsoft and seen a tremendous difference. The Apple culture is insular. People there didn't talk to the marketplace and were generally unaware of what was happening there.

I remember a meeting when we were trying to get Apple enthusiastic about our products as a way to help households decide to buy computers. Of the three Apple people in the meeting, it was clear who the senior person was. He was very knowledgeable about the difficulty consumers had purchasing computers. The other two weren't in touch with the market. At the end of the meeting we exchanged business cards and found out that the person who really knew what was going on was the summer intern—it was the Apple execs who were clueless.

What advice would you give to a startup company that doesn't have the marketing budgets to do in-depth surveys?

You don't need marketing budgets. The most important thing is to get your people to talk to customers. It costs you nothing but telephone charges. The worst thing to do is to have some survey company do the survey for you and then give you numbers. The most important thing is for you and the developers to talk with customers.

[*At this point in time, Eric Dunn, VP of Intuit's Personal Finance group, walked past us in the Intuit courtyard. Cook called out to him.*]

Eric, how many of your engineers in the past year have visited customers directly or interviewed them over the phone?

ERIC: Over 80 percent. Probably closer to 100 percent.

That is remarkably high for a Silicon Valley company.

It's the most important thing. Initially, we spent nothing on market research because we just had our people spend time on the phone interviewing customers, spending time with them at work, and spending time watching them in usability tests—just sitting there and taking notes.

Okay, but despite your initial market research, Intuit struggled because it tried to sell the Quicken product through banks. Wasn't it out of desperation that you placed ads targeted directly at consumers?

Not quite. We were in a business where competitors were spending and losing millions of dollars marketing their products. We had no money. One of our competitors invested, and lost, over seven million dollars in two years. We couldn't even raise $200,000. We did work with financial institutions for a while, but we knew that people bought their software from computer stores. Ultimately, we had to find a way to crack that channel or we'd remain a tiny company.

That's when we learned to get good at direct advertising. That raises another issue: companies must figure out what core competence they need to get good at. There are generally one or two things that you must be really good at in order to grow and flourish. At that point in time we had to get good at generating demand through advertising. Since we couldn't afford a sales force to cover the hundreds of thousands of stores around the country, I got some people to teach me direct response advertising. We were sick and tired of running a little company and wanted to either grow the business or get out. We took all the money we had saved from working with financial institutions and plowed it into advertising. Then I managed to get a distributor to carry the product and it worked. But none of this would have worked if the product hadn't been designed right. And the product wouldn't have been designed right unless we had understood the customer.

A really key thing for a growing company is to establish a repeatable process. Establish and set the culture so employees can repeat the success. If you can't keep repeating the successes, naturally you will flame out. The most important thing in growing the company is to build the culture and people so they achieve success on their own. It's important to distinguish between entrepreneurs and entrepreneurial companies. Often entrepreneurs are so accustomed to making the decisions themselves they end up creating anything but an entrepreneurial company. No one else in the company feels entrepreneurial except for the entrepreneur because the entrepreneur is telling everybody what to do. As an entrepreneur, you can't grow a sustainable company unless you can duplicate yourself. Others in the company must become entrepreneurs and push the business forward since you are typically stuck doing only what you comprehend. In my case, it's not very much.

The most important thing I and Bill Campbell do [Intuit's current CEO] is to grow the values and the people of the company. Our legacy is that, when we are dead and gone, the company can keep flourishing, growing, and applying the principles in ever-larger and more important ways.

Give us an example of how these principles translated into a successful product created by many Intuit employees.

With Quickbooks [Intuit's product for businesses], we repeated in the business accounting market what we did with Quicken in the consumer market. First, a team of our people went and understood the customer's needs. We found out that the existing accounting software companies totally misunderstood the key requirements of the majority of small businesses. Based on this, we invented a new kind of product and suffered huge, massive flaws in the product introduction. Do you know this story?

No.

This is fun. Accounting was about the oldest software category for PCs and we were just entering the market.

The example I'm setting up isn't about marketing flourish. Some people think, because of my Procter & Gamble background, I focus only on stuff like PR and advertising. This is an example of how useful those things were. We entered the accounting software business in 1992 amidst twenty-plus competitors, some of whom sold complete accounting software products for $49. We introduced our product without a price advantage; we sold it for $99. We introduced it without a known brand name or novel promotion. We advertised, but the first ads we ran were lousy. They were the worst ads we had ever run. I can say that because I helped write the first one. We had an ad agency do a second ad campaign for us and that turned out to be the worst ad we've ever run in the company's history. We got four responses to an expensive two-page color ad.

It was a pretty bad-looking ad.

Right. The ad was done in a *National Inquirer* format with a bald-headed lady and a family on pogo sticks. The agency thought that accounting was so dull they needed to grab people to get them to read it.

The ads were a disaster. Not only that, the product had bugs which caused your data to disappear. You'd spend a week typing the data and, poof!, it was gone. If it could have gone wrong on the launch, it went wrong.

But let's look at market share. The first month that we launched the product, it became the leading accounting software in the country and has remained number one. That's like introducing a new soft drink and having it pass as Coke. It was unbelievable, unfathomable. But it clearly wasn't the market launch that did it. The point is that we nailed the product and we nailed the service. We really had great, caring service.

There are two parts to the product offering, the customer service and the product itself. The only reason we were successful is that we had fundamental insights into customer behavior that competitors had missed. That's an example of duplicating a successful process and enabling the rest of the organization to lead.

How do you instill these values in your people? Is it by just hiring smart people?

That's part of it. The scary thing about entrepreneurial companies is that they grow up to be reflections of their founders. Unlike kids, where you can blame genetics, you hired all the people in your company. They follow your lead and, if they don't work the way you want them to, it's your fault—not theirs. It's up to you, the founder, the entrepreneur, to create the culture you want. Employees learn this more from your behavior than from your words. So you must model the behaviors that you want them to follow and internalize.

Inc. magazine called me up to say they wanted to write an article on all the tricks you must pull and corners you must cut to survive as an entrepreneurial company in this rough-and-tumble world. Shaving on ethics and things like that. I told them that I totally disagreed with their premise. If you do shave corners, all you accomplish is teaching your organization that that's how you win and that cheating is the right way to do it. You've now spawned a cancer far worse than anything you created. In my view, the only way to operate is to model the behaviors that you want your people to emulate. The same applies to decision making. If you want people to make database decisions, you must model database decisions. When employees can't make a decision and need your call, you can't just say, "I think it should be X. Go do it." This is great for an entrepreneur, but you are modeling that it's okay to make decisions by whim, as Apple did.

Let's move to competition. Everybody uses Intuit as an example of how a small company can compete against a larger company, i.e., Microsoft, and still manage to win. What's the story there?

I don't know, we've always competed against larger companies. I'd say that almost all entrepreneurs, by definition, compete against larger companies because the entrepreneur must start at zero. I'm not sure.

But Microsoft also paid a lot of attention to its customers.

They are good.

And seem as obsessively focused as you are. Given that, what was the distinguishing characteristic?

They are a good company. I have a lot of respect for them, obviously; we were willing to join up with them. You must simply have a manic focus on delivering the best to the customer and taking the best ideas wherever you find them. One of our values is "Seek the best." We want the best people and we want the best ideas, wherever they are. The most junior person in the company is often a great source of new ideas.

Yet, as you said before, if one of your much larger competitors had lifted their pinky, Intuit would have been history. Were they simply inept?

Why did the accounting software companies not recognize that two-thirds of small businesses don't know a debit from a credit to save their life and don't want to learn accounting? These are the customers who think that general ledger is a World War II hero.

So the competition never bothered to ask, and you did?

As far as I can tell. The most important thing to keep focused on is putting the customer first. When we pass out profit-sharing bonuses I tell employees that the check comes from Intuit, but the money comes from our customers. All the money we have comes from them.

I'll give you a simple example to show you what customers value. Let's say there was a mad bomber and let's imagine that he blew up my and Bill Campbell's offices. Would customers care? No, they wouldn't know and they wouldn't care. On the other hand, if that mad bomber hit the phone system in one of our customer service centers, within two minutes customers would know and within five minutes they would really care. So who is more important? If you are on an airplane do you really care what CEO Gerald Greenwald of United Airlines does? Not too much. You really care about what the people serving you do. That's the moral truth of business and it demonstrates the importance of great people.

The manager's job is to create the kind of environment that gets great people excited about what they do. So excited they do great work. So excited they tell their friends Intuit is a great place to work. That's when you know you are doing it right.

Somehow it must be unsatisfying for people to hear you say that you beat Microsoft by just focusing on the customer. It would be so much more exciting if you had used a magic bullet.

We constantly learned and turned that learning into products faster than they would. There is no magic bullet in competition because if there was, the other folks would use it too. There are no patents on this.

How do you hire people who are focused on and effective at conducting customer research?

It's culture more than hiring. You want to hire people who are excited about what you are doing, but you must also ensure that the work excites them. Once employees get here, the company values are what allow them to learn what's important. Hiring people is fairly easy because there are great people out there who want to do great things, only companies stand in their way. That entrepreneur who tells everybody what to do causes people to not feel ownership, responsibility, or the joy of leading a business themselves. Great people want to do that. They know they've got great ideas, they don't want to be told what to do. They want to lead and, frankly, they should lead.

If they're leading, how do you define your job today?

It would be interesting to ask our people how they define my job. In some sense our people are my customers. My job is to make them as effective, productive, and successful as possible. So they are the ones to evaluate how well I do it.

How do you think they would define you?

I think they would say that I provide big direction, open doors, and make tough calls. If it were Bill Campbell and I together, they would add creating a winning organization, removing the frictions, and finally, enabling people to grow far faster than they ever dreamed they could on their own.

6

SANDY KURTZIG
ASK

Go For It!

Women who've both started and grown successful technology companies are hard to find in today's computer industry. Women who accomplished this in an even more male-dominated industry in the 1970s are almost unheard of. We know of one—Sandra L. Kurtzig. She managed to sell her ware to large manufacturing giants while raising two sons. If we had to choose one word to describe this entrepreneur who built a $450 million company, it would undoubtedly be "moxie."

Kurtzig's interest in computers took hold while a sophomore at UCLA. She interned there for the summer in the university's computer center. Despite her complete lack of programming skills, she immersed herself in an attempt to solve her first major assignment—pinpointing the location of Eastern bloc radio waves bouncing off the ionosphere.

Kurtzig dropped out of Stanford's Aeronautical Engineering Ph.D. program with a master's degree and a yen for something more exciting than academia. By 1971, she found herself selling computer timeshare accounts for GE. At the time, the vast majority of businesses could not afford their own mainframes and instead rented time on others'.

On a sales call to a prospective client, her new company, ASK, was born. The customer, a telecommunications equipment manufacturer, needed custom software that tracked inventory, bills of materials, and purchase orders. After some thought, Kurtzig agreed to write this software, quit her job and received $1,200 for her work—a modest but sound beginning.

Kurtzig found that other manufacturers were also badly in need of her software for manufacturing management, called MANMAN. ASK blossomed as it expanded its product line and its base of customers.

Any entrepreneur with a growing company inevitably faces the decision to sell the business to a larger concern or continue alone. Kurtzig arrived at this crossroads in 1976 when Hewlett-Packard (HP) made a $1 million offer for ASK to sell the rights to its software. Kurtzig's negotiating counterpart was a young Ed McCracken (who would later go on to head Silicon Graphics). McCracken was less than thrilled at the prospect of having to go outside HP for programming talent. The frosty relations between the two didn't help matters. Determined to demonstrate her young firm's programming superiority, she spurned the offer and worked harder than ever to grow little ASK into an industry leader. HP was never as successful as ASK in providing a manufacturing software package of its own.

Confident in ASK's stellar ascent, Kurtzig abdicated CEO duties in 1985 to raise her two children. She remained as chairman until 1989 when her firm's revenues exceeded $185 million.

Less than a year into her retirement, ASK's board of directors persuaded her to rejoin as CEO to shepherd the company through increasingly turbulent waters.

Kurtzig repositioned the firm as a database provider and took her company to $450 million in 1992 revenues. Again, comfortable that her company was back on track, she retired to let professional management take over. Two years later, ASK was purchased by Charles Wang's firm, Computer Associates, as part of its acquisition strategy. All ASK products are now sold under the CA label.

We met with Kurtzig in her private office along Sand Hill Road in Menlo Park, California, home to most of the top Silicon Valley venture capital firms. Her office, easily the most ornate of any of those we interviewed in, oozed refinement and wealth. Our interview took place while we unhurriedly sampled coffee from elegant china cups.

"How many times have you seen a product in the market and said, 'I had that idea.'?"

You moved from an idea to a company in an unusual way. Tell us about it.

The company started as a part-time job in the second bedroom of my apartment. I started with $2,000, unlike many other entrepreneurs who had a lot of venture capital. I clearly didn't have a grandiose plan for creating a half-billion dollar company. I just wanted to produce some grandchildren for my parents, because they were getting on my nerves about giving them some grandchildren. I wanted to keep my mind active, so I thought I could have children and do something to supplement the family income and keep my mind occupied. So it started as a part-time job in the second bedroom.

I had read a lot of business journals. I read that American manufacturing companies were among the least productive of the industrialized nations and I thought to myself that it was because those manufacturing companies were only using their computers for payroll. It's important to pay your employees, but I realized that computers could serve greater needs in a manufacturing company. My first customer told me, "I really need something to track inventory and provide manufacturing information in a timely way." I thought that he was probably similar to a lot of manufacturing folks. After I developed the first series of software for that first customer I went to a second company and said, "Can I help you computerize your manufacturing operation?"

It was at this point that you started sending out flyers advertising your services?

Right. The second company said, "We also need to organize our manufacturing operations and keep track of inventory, but we're very different from the first company you worked with. Nothing you did there applies here." I said, "Well, tell me about your business." I would listen a lot to their problems. I realized that the problems of my customers—although *they* thought they were very dissimilar—in fact were very similar.

I took the base of what I wrote for the first customer and enhanced it with all the little nuances that were different for the second customer. Of course, I charged the second customer as if I started from scratch, because he thought he was unique. I didn't want him to think that he wasn't. I installed the software for the second company; they were very happy. I went to a third company, and the same thing happened. The customer said, "We're very different from the other ones. We're successful because we do everything differently." I listened to his problems and realized that again there were many more similarities than dissimilarities, even though there were some unique things he was doing.

I again used the base product and embellished and enhanced it. We became the first company to really develop standardized software as opposed to custom software. At the time, it was considered very innovative to be standardizing software. We started developing standardized software for the minicomputer market, specifically the manufacturing segment—financial and manufacturing applications in the manufacturing segment. That's how the company began.

The key was just listening to customers' problems, and then designing software. I did all the selling, and the collecting of money—I was sort of a one-man band. But two things happened. First, I never considered myself to be the best programmer, but my strength was in understanding what it took to write a program. I could communicate with very skilled programmers in terms of what was needed in the program. Also, by listening to my customer, I was able to learn enough about his manufacturing process to translate what he said, and think through the design issues. I was able to communicate what was needed to the programmers. My best skill was identifying the problem, translating the problem to the technical people, and understanding enough of each. I was also very hands-on. I did all of the bookkeeping at first, even though I didn't have a business background.

In growing the company, I knew enough about all the areas of the company, so when I started hiring people, I quickly knew whether they were BS-ing me or whether they were doing a good job.

Whether the job was investing money or banking, I was very hands-on and felt it was like "take the heat or stay out of the kitchen." You shouldn't have employees doing anything you wouldn't do. So I'd work very long hours, and so forth. I never said "just give me some people to do this" and then be hands-off. I was very involved. At the same time, I realized that I couldn't do everything by myself. So when I hired people I recognized that they weren't going to do their work exactly the way I would. But, even if they did it 90 percent, they would do many things better than I could. I could only do so much. So I was very willing to give people responsibility, authority, and let them work with it. So, I delegated. My attitude has always been that people are basically good.

That's a good attitude. Why is it unique?

It's a different attitude than a lot of companies around here have. A lot of bosses are very scared about hiring good people, because they think someone above will decide that the good people should get the promotions, not them. I've always felt that it's the good people around me that made me look good. It's definitely not threatening to me to hire people that are good. The way I see it, you always want to hire your replacement.

I was very concerned about giving up a big percentage of the employees' company, because they would think they no longer had control. If you're really out to create a big company, the first thing you should do is have the best people. If you want the business to be a success, whether you're running it or not is academic. If you're good, everybody is going to keep you in control. That's for sure. If you're not good, then you want someone else in control to make you rich.

In your case, you were in control.

I was, but it wasn't because of control. I never thought, "Is this company ever going to be worth anything?" I didn't have any venture capitalists, which was both good news and bad news. The fact that I didn't have venture capitalists meant I could make every mistake in the world without anyone looking over my shoulder. I would never have to say I was sorry. It was my neck on the line, no one else's. I think that allowed me to make a lot of mistakes.

No venture capitalist would have given me any money at the beginning. First, I was a woman. Second, the product was software and in those days, software had no value. It was difficult. Today, I would do it differently, but I would do it differently because of who and where I am now. If I went back to that time again, I would probably do it the same way again. It's as I said before: get as far as you can without outside money, because you don't really need a lot of money at the beginning when you're developing software. When we went public, I still owned 90 percent of the company.

When we first gave stock options to employees, they put them on the bulletin boards and they used them for dart practice. One Thanksgiving, ASK gave people turkeys. The employees didn't like it, so the next Thanksgiving I gave them some stock, and they thought that was worse than the turkeys. There were comments like, "This is really a turkey, giving stock" or "What's this piece of paper? This is ridiculous." Our lawyer said he knew that ASK was a real company when the stock options started coming off the dart board. For most of the people you're talking to, there wasn't that much money around. We all managed through hard times, as well as good times.

What concerns you about today's managers?

I'm concerned that a lot of today's managers haven't managed through the down times. There was an article this weekend in the newspaper about skyrocketing housing prices. It's very nice that everybody's gotten rich around here, but it's paper wealth. There are a lot of people running companies in Silicon Valley who haven't had the experience of managing through both up and down markets.

Is it that they lack the toughness to persevere?

They don't know if they have the toughness. They've never had to face it. They've only had up markets.

Some people think that there isn't going to be a down market. Steve Jobs said that the computer industry is going to just blast off; that this phenomenon is just the beginning.

I'm not saying they're not good companies, but nothing's worth the kind of multiple at which a lot of these companies are trading. In my mind, multiples are determined by the expectation of a company's growth rate into the future. So if your multiple is thirty, investors expect your earnings to grow at about 30 percent per year. That's a rough estimate.

When a stock sells at a 60 P/E multiple, do you think this company is going to grow for 60 percent per year into the future? You can't grow a company for very long at that kind of rate if you have to hire new people—even if they're standing in line and you don't have to interview them. You can go from one million to two million; that's a hundred percent growth. Two million to three million is really fifty percent. You just can't do that. As you grow, you can't sustain growth at the rates the stock market is currently expecting. It's unrealistic. You probably can't grow, realistically, at much more than a 25 or 30 percent rate. Look at Intel; look at Hewlett-Packard. These companies are growing at those rates, and their P/Es are in the teens or low twenties. And those are great companies. Those are companies I can invest in and sleep at night. Their P/Es are about the market average.

Let's move to the topic of ASK. Early in the company's life, you received what was essentially a buyout offer from Hewlett-Packard. How did you make the decision not to sell?

That was a weird deal. HP realized that software for the manufacturing industry was a good industry and they recognized that our software could help them sell a lot of hardware, mainly because they'd been trying to get into the Boeing account for years and couldn't. Data General and DEC were way ahead of them. And here we were, this no-name company that got a big deal with Boeing, and our software turned out to be the beginning of the relationship that HP had with Boeing. HP sold Boeing millions of dollars worth of LANs and millions of dollars worth of hardware. And, they recognized that our software could be a key for them, but we alone were not big enough to pursue all the places HP wanted to be.

Ed McCracken [then on the HP negotiating team and now CEO of Silicon Graphics] is the only person I have anything negative to say about with regard to this negotiation. In all fairness to him, he says it's a good thing that the deal didn't happen because ASK went on to such success. HP and ASK basically had an agreement where HP was to buy the software or buy the company. They had one price in mind and I had another price in mind, which was double theirs. To me, these were big numbers. When we had our pseudo-final negotiations with McCracken and Paul Ely [then HP Vice President], Ed started the conversation by saying, "I don't know why we should give these little kids anything. We have all these fantastic, brilliant HP engineers that can write all this software." That didn't start the conversation off on a good note. I don't know whether it was a negotiating strategy on Ed's part to get the perceived price down, or whether he honestly felt that way. I said, "You guys can't write this software in nine months." Paul Ely said, "We're going to do this in nine months with or without you, and we just want the software. Why don't you come design the software for HP?"

I replied, "You're not going to do this in nine months. It'll take you three years." End of HP negotiations! And of course, it took them much longer than three years. ASK kept staying ahead of the game. In software applications, you keep adding to application software and create a barrier to entry. The rest is history. We ended up becoming the largest purchaser of Hewlett-Packard computers. Instead of HP bringing us in with our software, we convinced them that we wanted to OEM [Original Equipment Manufacturer—essentially an arrangement between a supplier of a technology and another company which, in turn, adds its own logo and product name to the product for eventual resale] their hardware because we were doing all the selling work. That was also a unique arrangement, because until then, OEM meant a hardware OEM—that you added value with hardware. I said that adding value were the operative words, and we added value with software. At that time software was not considered an added value.

It was a gut move on both our parts, but HP is a classy company. Our choice to write software for the HP machine—part of it was by accident, part of it was that they were right in our backyard—was very key to our success. They were such a good and classy company and they wanted to be fair.

If McCracken had offered what you wanted, would you have taken it?

If they had offered $2 million, yes, absolutely. What you don't know about the future doesn't hurt you. At that point the money was more than I could ever imagine.

What role has luck played in ASK's success? Is it the dominant force in your case, or is it skill?

Al Shugart [founder and CEO of disk drive maker Seagate] once teased me when we were both giving a speech together. He said something like, "Luck's more important than your mother and Sandy will talk about luck." The role of luck has always been an inside joke on the peninsula, but I think you make your own luck.

I think luck is seizing opportunities. There are opportunities all around. There are millions of good ideas, but it's those people who seize the ideas and seize the opportunities that appear lucky. When you see an opportunity in the market, are you lucky that you see an opportunity? I think it's the seizing which is the key. There are plenty of brilliant ideas. It's those people who take those brilliant ideas and make a company that make the difference and, of course, reap the rewards of success.

How many times have you seen a product in the market and said, "I had that idea." It happens every day. You really have to go for it to be in business for yourself.

Would you consider yourself to be someone who is driven and seizes opportunities at every juncture?

I used to be.

Would you define yourself as someone who is willing to take incredible risks?

I don't see them as incredible risks. I don't think any entrepreneur would say that what they did was an incredible risk. I think most could tell you many reasons why it was obvious to do what they did. When you have nothing, you have nothing to lose; you haven't that far to fall. That's why so few entrepreneurs can do it a second time.

Because they've already made it and have much more to risk?

Once you've done it, you don't want to eat hamburgers anymore when you're used to eating steak. In order to do a startup you have to be willing to get down and dirty. Even Jim Clark didn't really start Netscape. He identified these smart guys with the technology. That's the way you can do it. Or Steve Jobs with Pixar; he saw a product, saw that the idea was good, and financed the idea. It's the only way you can really do it successfully the second time around because you need other people who are very hungry and are willing to take the risks.

What is your life like after ASK? Do you miss working there after devoting so much of yourself to it?

My case is a little unusual. My initial business idea was to start a family and have a part-time job. I didn't quite succeed at that idea since I was working 20-hour days. To make anything successful I think you have to work 20-hour days. Also, 65 percent of my business was outside the United States, so there was a lot of traveling in my work. I felt that I could always go back into business if I wanted to, but I couldn't turn back the clock and spend more time with my children. On my gravestone I'd like written, "Mother of Andy and Kenny"—not "Mother of Silicon Valley" or "Mother of MANMAN."

I left ASK both times because I wanted to spend time with my children. Luckily my children are turning out great—so far, anyway. It's been an enjoyable time. It's very hard for entrepreneurs who turn their companies over because there aren't really any successes after owners turn their companies over to someone else. I think that Apple fell apart because no new products were developed. The last time a good product was developed, other than Newton—which was a failure—was when Steve Jobs was there.

But HP managed to evolve and grow after Bill Hewlett and David Packard left.

Yes. HP was, is, very unusual. HP has definitely carried on the culture of Packard and Hewlett. I think if Gates left Microsoft the company would go on for a while, but it wouldn't be a stock you'd want to hold for too long. The same is true with Ellison and Oracle. I think there was a good transition at Intel because Andy Grove and Gordon Moore are still there. It'll be interesting to see what happens when Grove and Moore retire. It's very difficult. The entrepreneurs you are interviewing have created a culture. For better or for worse, the CEO sets the culture. That's the main job. Employees who have come to that company have chosen to live by that culture. In the case of HP you see that culture pervasively instilled throughout the organization, no matter where you go in the world. Then a new CEO came in. John Young, as much as I like him, didn't quite instill that same culture that Hewlett and Packard did.

So yes, I miss the company. I'm very proud of its reputation for producing good products and good customer service and being a good place to work. On the other hand, there are other things in life than ASK and working 18- to 20-hour days.

If you were starting over would you go back into manufacturing management software or would you read journals and consider going into other industries?

Would I go into manufacturing software? No, for the wrong reason. I wouldn't because I'm sort of bored with it. I've done it for twenty-some years. But I think there's still an incredible opportunity with the transition in technology. We succeeded during the transition from mainframes to minicomputers. Now there's a transition from minicomputers to client/server, and a transition from hierarchical databases to relational databases, and transitions from line-by-line user interfaces to GUIs [Graphical User Interfaces, e.g., Apple's MacOS or Microsoft Windows]. There's incredible opportunity in the market. Some of the new companies have done well. There's more opportunity today in manufacturing software than there ever was before. So, the answer is I'm bored with manufacturing software; I probably wouldn't do it over again, but I think there's still an incredible amount of opportunity in that market. There are other markets that I think are exciting. One is software for healthcare information systems. It has all the makings of a boom market for all the same reasons: transitions in markets and transitions in the industry itself. Any software that was written a few years ago is obsolete.

My number-one piece of advice for would-be entrepreneurs is to go for it. I'd say the top things are:

- *Believe in yourself.* If you don't believe in yourself, no one else is going to believe in you. You're not going to be able to communicate well if you don't believe in your idea.

- *Surround yourself with good people.* Have a good team and don't be afraid to share the glory and the responsibility and the authority. It takes a lot of hard work, and as the company gets bigger, it doesn't take any less. The work is just different.

- *Be willing to make mistakes.* You just have to make a few less mistakes than your competition.

- *Don't get wrapped up in your success.* When we went public all of a sudden we were the fair-haired children of the peninsula and we were the overnight success. But it took six or seven years of hard work and 20-hour days to become the overnight success.

- *You're still the same person you were when you started.* You still stand in line at the post office, you still put your pants on one leg at a time, and just because all of a sudden everybody thinks you're great, don't let it go to your head. If you do, when your business has a problem, you won't be able to cope with it.

7

JOHN WARNOCK/
CHARLES GESCHKE

Adobe Systems

ON PARTNERSHIP

The difficulty of starting a business by oneself is perhaps exceeded only by starting one with a co-founder. Capability, money, and ego almost invariably conspire to tear asunder any hint of a previously well-oiled partnership. In some cases the split is both planned and beneficial. More often, the divorce threatens to undermine the venture itself. With the exception of Hewlett and Packard and perhaps Gordon Moore and Andy Grove of Intel, no other duo has managed to withstand the rigors a technology startup faces and operate with such hand-in-glove efficacy as John Warnock and Chuck Geschke, the co-founders of Adobe Systems.

Geschke hired Warnock to the famed Xerox PARC in 1978. Their research derived advanced graphics capabilities and led the development of graphics-imaging standards.

In the past, developers and users of personal computers struggled with the challenges of printing documents. Developers had to write different pieces of software for each printer on the market and users were often unable to make screen text appear the same on paper, a maddening problem.

Warnock and Geschke did away with all this by creating software that linked the printer and the computer in such a way that users could print to any connected printer and manipulate the text and images on the fly. It was this technology that helped create the "desktop publishing" industry of the '80s.

Like so many other innovative microcomputer technologies that emanated from PARC, Xerox saw no commercial value in their technology. Convinced otherwise, Warnock and Geschke went into business for themselves.

They arranged a meeting with Apple's Steve Jobs, then leading the Macintosh development project and in search of a hot new technology to showcase his new computer. Jobs reportedly offered them $1 million to bring their software, known as PostScript, and join Apple; they demurred. Adobe Systems was born.

Adobe leveraged its PostScript franchise by developing technically superior applications, acquiring companies with complementary products, and delicately treading between the competing interests of its two largest partners, Apple and Microsoft. Today, Adobe is on target to break $1 billion in yearly revenues. However, the internet's impact on the computer industry reorders Adobe's world. For a company that built a business on creating professional-quality documents, the paperless world of cyberspace poses some challenges to Adobe's continued growth and good health.

Warnock and Geschke's similarities extend to physical appearance and demeanor; both in their mid-fifties, bearded, and gray-haired, they are the very picture of unassuming Ph.D. engineers. Warnock, chairman and CEO, is often described by outsiders as the technologist of the two. Geschke, the firm's president, is known for focusing on the business and marketing aspects of the business.

We met with these two quiet giants in Warnock's modest first-floor office to better understand how they turned a professional friendship into the dominant force in desktop publishing.

"The fact that I'm an entrepreneur is just an accident of my situation."

When Adobe started, there were already two very large players, namely Microsoft and Apple, whose interests you had to balance between. How did you handle it?

W: How did we manage it? In licensing PostScript, Apple wanted a window of opportunity. So PostScript's early licensees were more complementary than competitive to Apple and that gave them a running start on the desktop publishing business. As they gained strength and others entered the market, we started licensing to more competitive companies.

In the '84–'85 time frame, we had a great relationship with Microsoft. Bill [Gates] was a very approachable guy and we had friends who worked at Microsoft.

At Apple we had a great relationship with Steve [Jobs]. The Macintosh was just hitting the street and there didn't exist the competitive atmosphere even though Apple's "1984" ad campaign positioned Mac versus PC as this very, very competitive thing. It felt that way from the Apple side but not from the Microsoft side.

G: Early in Adobe's life people advised us to go after the biggest computer manufacturer. Instead, we went with Apple, which needed us in order to establish a position in the market. By establishing a micro-industry within the computer business, we could then go to companies like IBM and Hewlett-Packard.

So your explicit strategy was to work with smaller, less established companies?

G: Right. We also recognized that, unless we established ourselves as a strong technology vendor, we would be in a very weak position to negotiate realistic licensing agreements with the likes of IBM or HP, and probably wouldn't have been able to create enough value in the company.

W: It was valuable to tell potential partners, "We have this very, very profitable business with Apple. If you want to license from us, it had better be with the same terms and conditions." Had we shot-gunned the market we wouldn't have been in a strong negotiating position.

The basis for this technology of yours was developed when you were both at Xerox PARC. PARC is famous for being a great research center that can't implement its technology. Is that why you left?

G: There are really two parts to the question. Many who've written books about Xerox PARC placed 100 percent of the onus on Xerox management. In truth, management deserves some of the onus, but not all of it. First, Xerox management had no technology background even though they were viewed by many as a technology company. Management consisted mostly of people from sales, marketing, or finance. Their body language when they visited PARC was to have their arms crossed in front of them—which you know is the defensive strategy—"I don't want to deal with this." You can fault Xerox management for simply not understanding the products. On the other hand, it would be incredibly unfair to take us researchers off the hook. We had built ourselves a wonderful sandbox there, and though we very much wanted Xerox to succeed, we weren't realistic about the difficulty of selling an idea in an organization. We learned more about how hard that is after we left Xerox. As a research group we were never disciplined, motivated, or trained to do that. As a result, it didn't happen.

   Technology travels with people. You can't just throw it over the wall and, because it's such a good idea, expect another engineering group to simply pick it up and run with it.

W: I joined Xerox in 1978—

G: Hiring John was my best hiring decision.

W: Chuck was at Xerox for ten years and I had been there four years when we left. I had been with a number of startups and came to Xerox Research with my eyes wide open. I said, "God, this is the world's greatest place to do research." It really was. Great equipment. Great people. You could learn more in one year at Xerox PARC than you could anywhere else in five years. It was unbelievable. But, after talking to some of the senior managers it became clear to me that there wasn't a path from the research organization into the product world. There was no mechanism. Xerox essentially built the research organization—*in toto*—with no communication paths to the rest of the company and basically said about us, "These guys will invent things." The respective cultures of the manufacturing and the research organizations were like night and day. And the researchers had no desire to—

G: —get their hands dirty.

How does a company devolve to that state of affairs?

G: I'm more interested in figuring out how not to devolve to that position.

W: I think it was obvious. Xerox was a copier company. It was making a ton of money. It had cash, it had the franchise, it had the patent protection. It was the only copier company in the world and had great advance planning: "What should we do with cash? We'd better invest in our future. Let's throw a ton of money at investing in our future without worrying about the cultural aspects." That caused PARC to occur.

G: It's something we all struggle with when we have an incredibly successful product. It's difficult to invest resources in something other than the successful product unless you can predict the new one will be at least as successful as the current winner. Well, it's hard to figure out where the next multi-billion-dollar business is. It's much better to create a few ten-million-dollar businesses and see which ones emerge. And that's a problem we struggle with here. We have some product lines here that are multi-hundred-million-dollar product lines but we can't put all of our resources in those businesses. We have to build new businesses. So we go develop products like Acrobat and use the profits and the successes in the other businesses to invest in the new ones.

W: But the culture of the organization must be united. Having a research organization with no connection to reality is, in some sense, doomed to failure.

G: Here we have what you would call a research group, our Advanced Technology Group. But those people often work on specific aspects of a product's technology and they work with it all the way until product delivery and they then recycle back to the development group. We purposely keep an easily penetrable membrane between the research and product groups.

So your researchers in Advanced Technology don't just hand it off to the folks in product development?

No.

One of the hallmarks of successful startups is their ability to adapt to their market situation. When you first wrote your business plan, the idea was to create a print shop business. How did you adapt?

W: Actually, there was the very first business plan, then there was the second business plan, and then the third business plan...

G: We never actually wrote the third business plan.

W: We were talked out of the first—starting service bureaus for printing and publishing. We thought that companies needed printed material and that we could combine laser printers with computers and take the companies' print jobs.

G: We were going to do PIP (Postal Instant Press) kinds of things.

Just a single store?

GW: It was going to be a whole franchise!

G: All this stuff we knew nothing about.

W: Right. And Bill Hambrecht [of the San Francisco investment bank, Hambrecht & Quist], rightly said, "You guys don't know anything about that business. It's a street savvy, down-and-dirty kind of business. You don't want to be in that kind of business."

G: We only had our two beards.

W: Hambrecht said, "You need to figure out something that leverages the technology. You're technologists." We said, "That's cool." At the time there weren't cheap laser printers. Laser printers were $20,000 items at that time and Sun Workstations were just coming out. We thought we had a huge opportunity by putting a Sun workstation together with a $20,000 printer and making publishing solutions for corporations. Boeing and Hughes had problems. All the big aerospace companies had big publishing problems. Six startups in 1982 tried to do this business model: Interleaf, Xyvision, Tekset, Qubix, Viewtec, and Kamex.

They're all gone now?

G: Interleaf is still around.

W: Xyvision may still be around. Kamex got swallowed up by Du Pont. About six startups had exactly the same business plans.

G: Which is why it was easy to raise money. It's always harder to raise money when you're alone with a product or service idea.

W: We raised two-and-a-half-million dollars with that business plan. We then hired our VP of sales and marketing and did the technical development for PostScript. Then we got the famous phone call from Steve Jobs.

G: In all fairness we got the first call from Gordon Bell [vice-president of engineering] at DEC. It turned out that he had the same problem that Steve had.

W: Gordon Bell visited and said, "We at DEC have probably spent ten to fifteen million dollars on projects trying to drive laser printers and nothing has worked. It's been a total bust. You know how to do this. You really should license your technology to corporations."

G: And we said, "Sure, but no thanks. We want to build computers."

Everybody was building computers at the time.

W: Then we got the call from Steve who said, "We could put your technology into a printer and drive it from the Macintosh." This got our attention. We realized that if we had a business licensing PostScript we wouldn't have to do manufacturing or build a big sales force, and would essentially get paid a pure royalty for our software. Our head of sales said, "Guys, this is obvious! You are getting two of the three legs of a business out of the way. You've got a pure technology play!"

G: It meant less money, but higher quality money—90 percent-plus margins.

W: And no cost of sales. This happened within the first four months of the company.

You turned down Jobs' million-dollar offer to hire you.

W: It was actually a five-million-dollar offer. He wanted to buy the company.

G: And he would call about once a month during the contract negotiations and say, "Doing this contract is a lot of nuisance. How about if I just buy you?"

Tell us about working with Jobs. There's this legendary "charisma" that is often referred to.

W: It's very real. Absolutely. He is one of the great natural leaders. He can motivate people like no one I've ever seen.

G: If it weren't for Steve, we wouldn't be having this conversation. He did more for us than just doing the deal and getting the development resources inside of Apple.

At one point some people at Apple realized that they were trying to sell a printer that cost twice as much as their Macintosh computer. I remember a gut-wrenching meeting with the head of marketing at the time, Mike Murray, and Bob Belleville, head of development. They basically told us that our project wouldn't see the light of day. When they left I called Steve and told him that we heard that Apple had decided not to do the product. And he said, "Hell no. We're going to do it." It was his drive that brought the product to market even though most of Apple's senior management thought it was madness.

W: This is a great story. I got this call one day. [*In a high-pitched voice*]: "Hi, this is Steve Jobs. I hear you're really doing some great stuff over there. We'd like to come see you."

So we said, "Ohhh-kay."

Steve came and said, "We've tried to do this for a couple of years and we can't do crap. What we ought to do is figure out how to take your technology to our machine."

G: So we had a breakfast at the local Good Earth restaurant, which is where he negotiated all of his initial deals.

W: We talked about getting acquired, about working together, and I think we all just formed a friendship. They gave us two-and-a-half-million dollars for about 20 percent of the company and gave us a one-million-dollar advance against royalties.

I remember the contract meeting with Apple CEO John Sculley, board member Al Eisenstadt, and Jobs. Eisenstadt said, "Let me get this straight. We're giving this no-name company—they haven't even been in business a year—a million-dollar advance plus two-and-a-half-million dollars in cash. We have no guarantee that they can deliver and we're doing this just on pure faith?" And Steve said, "Yup. That's right." So they invested in us in preparation for a 1985 product launch.

Let's talk about Adobe's growth. Much of it has been by acquisition. To what extent did you pay attention to cultural issues while integrating Aldus?

G: A lot.

W: Actually Aldus' culture wasn't that similar to Adobe's.

G: —At the senior management level.

W: It really wasn't. It's a difficult problem. It doesn't work to decide that you can operate two companies separately and get synergies from them. You must take dramatic steps to acculturate the acquired company.

G: We took a couple of our most capable, young managers and moved them to Seattle in order to personally introduce the Adobe culture.

How exactly were the two companies' cultures different?

W: Aldus' CEO, Paul Brainerd, acquired companies but left them as different units, with different marketing departments and different sales departments. They were self-contained little businesses. They lived and died on their own.

I think that when you buy little companies like that, they generally fail. In Aldus, we inherited all of those little companies.

Wasn't it almost a merger of equals in terms of company size?

W: Yes. In terms of number of employees. Not at all in terms of profitability.

If your senior management teams didn't get along, how did you keep them on board?

We didn't. John Young, the former Hewlett-Packard CEO, said that if you acquire a company, take the first layer of management out.

Was that difficult?

W: No. They had great severance packages. We kept one, a very valuable employee who ran their European business.

G: We selectively kept people. There's almost no other way to do it and still achieve the needed integration. It's not because people are not bright enough or capable enough. It's just that they've been accustomed to being senior management and all of a sudden they've become a relatively smaller piece of the puzzle. It just doesn't work.

You can do it in a humane way. John sounds like a tough guy but he's not. He's a pussycat.

W: When Computer Associates acquires a company, they are fairly brutal. They just go in and take the employees out. They say, "OK folks, you guys will be staying and you guys will be leaving."
   Aldus just thought about things differently from us. They said that we would never make PageMaker a 25 percent pretax (profit) business—that it couldn't be done. We had it running that way in the first couple of quarters.

G: It's just a different way to focus the business.

W: Focus the business, focus the resources, and leverage things. I would say the Aldus merger is done. There are still residuals where the culture is different, but it's diminishing.

Let's talk a bit about the challenges you face today as a large corporation.

G: You mean our high-flying stock.

We all hear about a total paradigm shift to the internet. Do you see a paradigm shift?

G: Yes. I think we're better positioned to take advantage of that paradigm shift than anyone else in the business. I know that *Business Week* spends a lot of time telling you how Microsoft has sorted it all out. But we've been sorting it out for the last three years. We invested in Acrobat in expectation that the world would shift toward moving information electronically. Like everybody else, we had no magic knowledge about the internet and the speed at which it was going to grow. But implicitly, not just by dumb luck, we were investing in the technology that can leverage the internet.

W: I totally agree with Chuck. It's all about moving information. The internet is about the exchange and movement of information.

Your co-management approach to the company is unique. Aside from the David Packard-Bill Hewlett partnership, you two are the only consistently well-working team of any of the giants. What's your secret?

W: I don't know if either of us could verbalize it.

G: As I said, John was my best hiring decision ever. From the day I first met him, we've respected one another's intellectual capability, inherent honesty, ethical behavior and principles by which we lead our personal and business lives. You can't recruit for that. Our partnership happened by accident. The result is that we've known each other for almost twenty years now and have never really had a serious argument. It doesn't mean we always agree. I'm sure once in a while we'll bruise each other's ego, but the value of our friendship is so much more important—we get our egos out of the way.

W: If I'm out of town, there isn't a company decision that I wouldn't trust Chuck to make.

G: As a result, we've been able to lead reasonably rational lives outside of work as well. We've both had trophy wives for over 30 years. To me that means so much more than anything else. But our friendship is unusual.

W: When we started the company we made the fundamental decision to always be compensated identically.

G: Actually I get a little more than John because I'm a year older and have a higher insurance cost.... I think I make $100 more a year.

W: We really are complementary. We've never had a major disagreement about the philosophy of running the company.

Ever?

Ever.

Not once?

W: Not once. In terms of important values we simply track together.

So your secret might be in not turning every small decision into a big disagreement?

G: If one of us makes a decision that the other would have done differently, you must decide if it's important enough to cause a scrap.

W: I won't make a major decision without asking my buddy.

G: If the decision doesn't sound OK we make a slightly different decision. That's key: you don't make random decisions and then expect the other person to endorse them.

Can you give us an example of how you split your duties?

W: We both do what we like.

That arrangement doesn't create excessive overlap?

G: There is overlap.

W: It overlaps, but as I say, I won't make a decision without asking Chuck and Chuck does the same. If we do overlap we get consensus beforehand. If we've had disagreements they've probably been over individual personnel issues. I might like someone more than Chuck will or Chuck will like someone more than I do.

G: People really want to find a difference in what we do. So they say John's the technologist and I'm the businessman. And it's bull-shit, just bullshit. But if it makes them feel good, fine.

John tends to focus much more on product design. I have a longer attention span than John. The joke at Adobe was that if you wanted to get John's attention, you had to bring a hammer and nails and nail his shoes to the floor, or he would go away. Sure, we have different personalities. We're not the same person. But we both do well in front of customers and spend a lot of time on the road visiting our remote offices. I visit our office in Japan three or four times a year—a bit more than John. John spends more time dealing with the engineering people on new technology.

So yes, there are complements. But when push comes to shove, if necessary, we can pretty much completely replace each other.

W: Employees who have tried to divide and conquer us politically have always failed.

You guys don't look like typical entrepreneurs. You are Ph.D.s, Xerox PARC researchers, you are older than most entrepreneurs...

G: I can take my beard off.

Physical appearances aside, do you consider yourselves entrepreneurs?

G: People call us entrepreneurs. I don't think of myself that way. I don't think of myself as a businessman even though I know I must be one. I don't compartmentalize myself that way.

What keeps you coming to work at Adobe?

G: The reason I come to work every day is that I work with a group of people in an organization that can impact and change the world. That's what motivates me. If being President of the United States motivated me, maybe I would have done that instead, although I could never get elected. The fact that I'm an entrepreneur is just an accident of my situation.

Remember that the most frustrating thing at Xerox PARC was not getting that great technology out into the world. That drove most of us out.

Sheer frustration?

G: We had built beautiful products that nobody used.

W: It's sort of like a poet writing something that no one reads. Most programmers are driven by the prospect of impacting the market: "Hot damn. A million people use my code."

G: The first time someone extends their hand and says, "I want to shake your hand because the product you've made has changed my life," is the biggest sense of satisfaction you get. I don't know if that feeling is inherent in the entrepreneurial spirit, it motivates me more than anything else, by far.

W: The money and all of that stuff is nice, but it's not why we started Adobe. It just isn't the equation. The money is more a measure of how well you've run your business and the impact you've had on the market.

But if your reason for starting a business was changing the world, you could have accepted Steve Jobs' offer to hire you and avoided all the risk of starting your own firm.

G: My perception was that a universally useful technology couldn't be captive to a single organization. We had to publish what we were doing and had to get broad industry adoption. The printing and publishing world is 10–15 percent of most countries, GDP. I thought it was unrealistic that one company could spread the technology so widely.

W: We'd also just come out of Xerox, which totally botched the world's greatest technology. There was no guarantee that Apple wouldn't botch things. At that time we just wanted to take a shot at making a difference.

You've accomplished that much. What advice would you give to entrepreneurs today?

W: The same piece of advice we got from our early chairman of the board. He said, "If your company grows, it will hit multiple plateaus of growth. Your primary objective is to grow and to get yourself fired." In other words, stop doing the job you're doing and grow to the next level so that others can perform the work you were doing. Another way to say it is consciously recognize when you've hit a plateau and delegate effectively to let other people take over. I think 99 percent of company founders hit the wall because they don't make that transition and instead try to stay in control of their company.

G: The other piece of advice is to hire people smarter than you.

W: There's a management philosophy—the job of the managers we hire is not to be boss. A manager's job is to be an expediter, to amplify the power of his or her people and to bring out the best in them by getting them to communicate and solve problems without necessarily telling them what to do. Adobe's culture is not an authoritative, autocratic, high-structure kind of thing where I tell you what to do. It's just not that kind of place. Much of our success in a dynamic marketplace comes from having managers who know how to leverage people.

G: The other bit of advice I'd give to an entrepreneur is to hire people who are finishers. It's extremely important to envision what you want to accomplish and to reward people who actually ship the product. A lot of startup companies flounder because they are always working on an idea over the horizon.

It's always more enticing to chase rainbows.

G: Of course. That may be rewarded in some cultures.

Is there any way you can tell who's a finisher and who isn't?

Mostly by experience. At first, we tended to hire people we already knew. We didn't hire young people just so that we could pay them a lower salary. We hired the people we thought were the best.

W: Old graybeards. Seasoned professionals.

G: The early people were from Xerox or ARPA [Advanced Research Projects Agency]. Particularly the engineering people.

How large a part did luck play in your success?

W: A huge amount.

G: When we started this company we didn't know about Steve Jobs. We didn't know about the Macintosh. We didn't know Canon was going to bring out a cheap laser printer. We didn't know that computer memory prices were going to come down. We hadn't met Paul Brainerd. We didn't know any of that stuff. We had an idea and we were fortunate enough to bring it together at the right time.

W: It's not only really important at the beginning to be in the right place at the right time, it's incredibly important to develop not for what the market is today but what the market will be in two years' time. If you happen to be in a startup, you're lucky the first time you hit it and have a successful product. After that it's a matter of building the infrastructure to anticipate the future. For that, you must have talented individuals with insight and vision about how markets interact. So many companies are one-product companies. They have a hit, they grow, and they die.

G: Being smart and working hard are required for success, but they're not sufficient.

8

MICHAEL DELL

Dell Computer

GROWING TEXAS REIGN

At age 19, Michael Dell decided to drop out of the University of Texas to found his own computer company. Instead of becoming a doctor, lawyer, or engineer, the young freshman dropped out of college so that he could "compete with IBM." Was this a misguided, rash decision that only a teenager could make?

Perhaps Dell decided to drop out of school so that he could do what he loved: being an entrepreneur. Entrepreneurial spirit was a part of Michael Dell since his childhood. When Dell was 12, he devised a stamp auction that made him $1,000. And, during his senior year in high school, Dell earned $18,000 selling newspapers and bought a BMW—cash down. And, in retrospect, most people would certainly agree that Dell made the right decision. In Michael Dell's first year of business, his company's sales topped $6 million. All from selling computers.

Michael Dell, however, sold computers somewhat uniquely: he sold them directly to the customer. This means that Michael Dell didn't have a showroom when he sold computers. He sold them over the phone. He sold them from his dorm room; and he may have even sold them in his pajamas.

In fact, Dell was one of the pioneers of the direct-to-consumer approach. At the time of the inception of his company, computer dealerships were the primary way for a customer to purchase a computer. Dell helped revolutionize the idea that consumers could buy computers over the phone. By doing so, companies selling computers could gain higher margins through reduced overhead, and could offer the customer a better deal than retailers.

What resulted was a company that skyrocketed in growth. Starting from $6 million in 1984, Dell Computer grew to $69 million in 1987, to $546 million in 1991. Dell wanted to grow, grow, grow and kept doing so. But as the giant beanstalk began soaring to dizzying heights, something strange happened: according to Dell, the company "hit the wall."

Dell Computer began to unravel. Its chief financial officer resigned, and questions were raised over its accounting practices. More importantly, the company had to terminate all of its new lines of laptops because of poor communication and planning. Dark days were indeed upon Dell Computer, and its stock price plunged from $49 in January 1993 to $16 in July. Dell blames these problems on "growing too fast"—growing without laying the infrastructural tracks needed for such growth.

Dell prides himself on realizing this mistake quickly, and on rapidly changing the philosophy of the company. Consequently, the company quickly resurged, and today remains one of the towering leaders of the PC industry. Dell Computer had revenues of $5.3 billion in 1996 and now employs more than 8,000 people.

Due to time considerations, we interviewed Michael Dell over the telephone.

"When you're making company decisions and driving a business, it doesn't matter if you're 22 or 42 or 82."

You are the youngest giant in our book. Has being much younger than the people you dealt with in business ever bothered you?

No, it's really never been a problem. I think that one of the reasons why it hasn't been a problem is because of some of the folks who came before me, that you also interviewed. So, having a young guy running a company was not so unusual in the technology industry.

Now, there are cultures where this is less likely to occur. For example, in Japan, age is a trait with which comes respect, intelligence, etc. So, a 25-year-old CEO of a company in Japan—well, something must be wrong here. You do get a lot of funny looks.

But, my view has always been that when you're making company decisions and driving a business, it doesn't matter if you're 22 or 42 or 82. We're just doing business.

But, at the same time, there certainly must have been people during your business encounters who questioned your ability to make decisions as such a young person. How did you deal with that?

I ignored them, basically.

(They laughed.) *But, if they are your customers, then you have to address them—*

Ah. Never happened with customers. Never happened with suppliers. Now, I'm sure behind closed doors, people were asking, "So, what's with the kid?" But, this doesn't happen anymore, because now I'm an old guy. [Dell is 32.]

When you were selling out of your dorm room—similar to the prototypical garage, except yours was a dorm room—you obviously didn't have a master plan to be a dominant PC vendor. At what point did you realize that you had the potential to create a very large business, and was this the reason why you left school?

I remember there was a point where I realized that I had the opportunity to sell in excess of a million dollars a month of computers, and that this was a very reachable goal without a lot of obstacles. That, combined with what I saw as an economic discontinuity with the retail computer dealers sprouting up all over the countryside with their high markups and low service, just appeared to be a basic opportunity.

My underlying thinking was to focus on economics first, and then the customer, and then the product—as opposed to product, customer, economics, which is the traditional way in our industry— and this kind of thinking has been fundamental to our success for a long time.

When you made a decision to leave school, were you absolutely confident you would sell over $1 million per month, or did that seem like a risk to you?

Well, it didn't really seem like a risk to me, because I was already earning obscene amounts of money for what, to me, appeared to be relatively simple work. The worst thing that could happen was that I would discover something that I didn't know at the time, and I would return to school.

In fact, I thought that the greater risk for me would be to *stay* in school, in case this opportunity disappeared while I was in school.

So, would you give the same type of advice to students who are deciding between finishing school and starting a company? Would you just tell them that they can go back to school later on?

That's a great question. And I've given the same answer many times, and that is: If I have to tell you, then you don't know.

The reason I say that is because I've been to these "entrepreneur meetings," and people ask, "Michael, tell me what I should do." And, I tell them, "Well, if I have to tell you, then you don't know."

This is not something you can put in the context of a rule-of-thumb. It's a very personal decision, and you have to have your own conviction, and if you don't have it, then you won't do it. If you do, then you will, and I don't have to tell you that.

Let's focus on this model of direct-to-consumers. Why didn't your competitors try this earlier? They clearly saw you making so much money— by eliminating overhead and offering customers a better deal. Why do you think they were so sluggish in responding?

Well, I think that in large measure they have underestimated the business model, and continue to do so even today. If you look in the archives of business publications, you'll see all sorts of this phenomenon. For example, in *Business Week* around 1988, there was a story about Dell at about the time we were going public. And a noted industry guru basically said that he didn't think we could grow beyond $150 million of sales. And now, that's about two days worth of orders. (*He laughed.*)

A lot of people just totally misunderstood what we were doing. I remember Rod Canion [the founder of Compaq] telling *PC Magazine* that he didn't compete with so-called "garage shop operations." It's a wonderful quote.

So, it's perhaps a snobbish view of Dell's business model, and second, maybe not being as close to customers and understanding their requirements.

Yes. Being detached from the customer is the ultimate death. And a lot of these guys—they think their customer is the dealer! Which is still amazing to me.

What kind of qualities do you look for when hiring new management people?

We've probably hired one senior person a month since the company has been in existence. And this has been because of the scaling of the business, and new markets, and the like.

The qualities we look for are data-driven, fact-driven people. Content experience. People who have a strong achievement ethic and have integrity, and know where risk should be taken, and where it should not be taken.

If experience is important, then if a young Michael Dell were to come to you today and tell you that he wants to be part of your senior team, is that pretty much out of the question because he doesn't have a proven track record?

Well, I would have never gone to work for a company! (*All laughed.*) I would have never imagined myself going to work inside of a corporation. Now, I'm very happy *running* a company—I like to create things and be involved in strategy, and there is plenty for me to do in that regard here. But, if I were 19 today, I would probably go start another business instead of going to work for a company.

Your track record before you were 19 would have led us to believe that—your stamp auction, newspapers, etc. Would you describe yourself as an entrepreneur?

Sure. But sometimes that implies that you're not a builder or developer. I think I've passed through a couple of stages of evolution here, and have been very comfortable in building and growing a business as opposed to starting and creating a business. But, at the same time, realize that we are creating things here all the time, because the business is so dynamic.

One of the skills you have down is selling. Do you think salesmanship can be developed, or do you think you've always been a good salesman?

Well, I'm probably not generically a good salesman, in the sense that I could sell anything. I think that I'm good at communicating the value of things that I think are genuinely valuable (*Dell laughed*), as opposed to just selling anything.

If you're good at "communicating the value of valuable things," do you think this skill can be developed or not? And if so, how?

I think it's almost like sharing the passion and the excitement. I've always believed that with a business this exciting, it's just a tremendously valuable resource to be able to tap into this. For example, inside a company, to motivate employees and get them excited, just ask them, "How many times do you get to be able to be part of creating a business? And how many times are you able to be a part of creating a business that is doing well?"

Can this be learned? Sure. Through examples and role modeling, and that sort of thing. I'm sure that there is some genetic influence, but I think that most of what I've learned is a function of the people that I've been around, including our customers.

If you think I came into this business with a master plan—we knew everything we were going to do in the next 12 years, and everything was all mapped out, and let's go do it... Wrong. We made lots of mistakes. But we corrected those mistakes really fast, and we often didn't make the same mistake twice. Or if we did, it wasn't fatal.

Speaking of mistakes, people would consider Dell's previous failed notebook launches and the repercussions of growing so quickly as perhaps the biggest test in the company's history. In retrospect, what could you have done better as a manager from that whole situation, and what did you learn from that?

Well, what we learned was that there *is* such a thing as growing too fast. I've asked a couple of suppliers and people we deal with that haven't gone through this, listening to them talk as I did many years ago—and ask them, "Can you grow too fast?"

And they won't tell you no. They have to experience it themselves before they figure it out. We grew 127 percent one year. There I am, cover of *Fortune* magazine, the 127-percent poster boy. This is killer stuff. You don't know you're going to have a problem until you hit the wall—and you hit the wall high-speed, and parts go flying everywhere. And, more growth, in this case, doesn't help you. Because it's just more confusion. We were at a point where the infrastructure just got totally outstripped.

So, I think what we would have done differently is to balance the growth with the infrastructure. Cash flow—at least in the business model we have, if you can keep your cash flow very positive, then this minimizes your risk dramatically. Profits—the whole infrastructure around information systems, and eventually building strong internal audit capability. Not the kind of things you learn about in high school. (*All laughed.*)

Which is about the extent of my preparatory education. I mean, I had macroeconomics in college, and I think I remember something about buy low, sell high. (*All laughed.*)

Do you ever look back and regret not finishing up your bachelor's degree?

No, not at all. I think I'm receiving a wonderful education. I haven't gotten my degree yet, but I'm learning tremendously, and growing, and the business offers all sorts of opportunity to learn new things every day.

You talked a lot about the fact that you don't want to grow just for growth's sake. If that's the case, then what is your metric for Dell's success?

Well, of course, even though we say we don't want growth for growth's sake, we are outgrowing all of our competitors. What we really want is growth combined with strong profits and cash flow. If you take the first-time consumer, you can sell a lot of computers to first-time consumers with low prices. You can also not make any money doing it. That's not a very economically redeeming or fun activity —

i.e., Packard Bell—

i.e., Packard Bell. And to us, economically redeeming and fun are the same things. We want to be in businesses where we can make money, and just growing a business without creating value for our shareholders, for our customers, and for the people inside the company—we don't think that that is a responsible way to run a business.

Most of the people we've spoken with said that when their company hit a speed bump, there were calls to have them removed as the CEO of their company. Did you face that?

Not really. I don't recall any real people outside the building chanting, or anything like that. Perhaps one of the reasons why that happened was that we were so aggressive in identifying the problems, communicating the problems, and addressing the problems in a very fast way.

We were very forward in saying, "OK, this is what we screwed up. This is what we did wrong. We shouldn't have done this. Here's how we are going to fix it. Here's what we think is going to happen."

And then, we overachieved on our recovery plan—you've got to give people a way forward to get out of things like this. If we had dug our heels in and said, "Oh, well it was the market, the economy, the recession, dog ate my homework..." Nonsense.

When a business goes wrong, look only to the people who are running it. That's my belief. And it was our fault. We screwed up. And we were very forward about saying that inside and outside the company. And there was a lot of support for the management team throughout this.

Someone once observed that one of the reasons why they thought Dell and Compaq were doing so well was because these companies were so competitive with each other, because each company had a target company to compete with. About a year before we had our problems, Compaq had a similar experience. And one of the things that inspired me was that 12 months later, everybody had completely forgotten about Compaq's previous problems. It was like it had never happened. And so I knew that all we had to do was to fix all of these problems, and 12 months later, nobody would ever think about it. And that's exactly what happened.

Regarding the future of the PC, some of the CEOs we've spoken with have spoken about how the network computer will become a standard household appliance, and how PCs are going to be defunct because of their non-user-friendliness. Even you have commented that computers are too hard to install and use. Do you see the network computer as being a threat to Dell's future?

Well, I think that the network computer, or set top box, or whatever you want to call it, is not in our view at all a replacement for the PC. There may be some incremental markets that emerge for people who want to have low adaptability, low flexibility devices that are in a different space than the PC.

For a company, you have two kinds of [computer] users: fixed and mobile. If you have a network computer, and you're in a mobile environment, like on an airplane, then you are out of luck. There's no connection. So you can't use a network computer on an airplane. Or in a train or in a car, because there is no local storage or processing.

Except, in some NCs [network computers], these things are included, and some of them have processors. And some of them look a whole lot like low-end PCs, and in fact, they cost a lot like low-end PCs, which brings up the whole question, "Why are you getting these to begin with?"

The other problem is that users will want to store their data on a big server somewhere and there is obviously a cost to that. If you are a corporate user and you have NCs and PCs, then you have to develop the applications twice, which adds cost.

Then, you have the whole bandwidth question. Your typical CD-ROM has about 500 megabytes, and the amount of data you are sending from the CD-ROM drive to the processor is huge.

Think about it this way. If you have a network, it's probably about a 10-megabit network today. Put [Microsoft] Powerpoint on one machine, and try running it from another machine over the network. It sort of works okay, you'd rather have it on your local disk, but it functions. Now, step down 10 times to a 1 megabit network, and try it. Well, it's absolutely unmanageable. You'd rather have a root canal. If you go down another 10 times, you're at ISDN—128 kilobits. There is absolutely no chance you can transmit that amount of data over an ISDN line.

So, the problem is that a lot of computing is data- and graphic-intensive. You go to the grocery store and your kid wants to get the CD-ROM from the latest Disney movie—well, if you don't have a high bandwidth interaction, you can't send that much data.

I've never run into a user who has logged onto the internet and has suddenly found that he needs less power now that he is on the internet. In fact, exactly the opposite occurs. You get on the internet, and you need more power. Here comes the screaming sound, faster network connection, larger monitor.

Here's a challenge for you. Get out your NC, and type www.disney.com. Pretty popular site. What you'll find is that there are just a tremendous amount of things on that site that are PC-centric—if you don't have a PC, you can't use them!

I think that what is really going on here is not that NCs are going to replace PCs. But rather, Silicon Graphics, Oracle, Sun, and IBM are all worried about one thing. And it's called Windows NT. And this is all just a smokescreen to try to distract the competitive issue that when Windows NT succeeds, it will do great detriment to the businesses of those four companies.

If you think about it, as you get Structural Dynamic Research and Parametric Technologies software on Windows NT dual-processor Pentium Pro workstations with 3D graphics, you've essentially gone right at the heart of SGI and Sun. When you have Windows NT succeeding, you have SQL Server succeeding, which is 80 to 90 percent of the functionality of Oracle's database at one-tenth the cost. When Windows NT succeeds, multiprocessor scalable Pentium processor servers succeed, which goes right at the heart of IBM's enterprise computing business.

I think that that's the *real* issue here.

What about the argument of simplicity, though? Americans really don't want complicated machines, and right now, computers are really complicated. And a set top box is going to be a lot easier to use.

I think that the manageability aspect is a valid one, and that is something that the industry has to address, because PCs are more difficult to use and more difficult to manage than they should be. And that's something we're all working on. But, I think that's the answer to this problem, not the NC.

What's been the proudest moment in your career?

Hmm. Well, sort of every day is the proudest moment. Every period of time you look, we have set and broken our own records. One of the things that makes me personally proud, or perhaps more happy than proud, is when I go over to see Dell in Australia or Singapore or Malaysia or Thailand. And based on a fairly simple idea and a business model, some really creative guys have managed to put this business model into a whole new country and it's *thriving*, all by itself. That's a very proud moment for me.

How do you think your role has changed as CEO from age 19 to now? What have been the major shifts in responsibilities?

The first couple of years of the company's life, I was directing tasks at a pretty detailed level, which is not unusual for a company that size. As the company grew, my focus increasingly became hiring talented people, putting an organization in place. Eventually, that evolved into a role of driving the company's strategy, helping to set the high bar in terms of what our performance objectives are. Helping to evolve the overall organization, who our partners are going to be outside, looking at the industry, understanding what customers are doing in an overall sense. But it's gone from highly operational task focus, do everything yourself because there is nobody else there, to a lot more fun job, which is to set the strategy.

In some respects, my job is a lot easier than it has ever been because there are so many talented people. Ten years ago we were struggling to cope with our growth. It is a lot harder when you don't have talented people, because you can't rely on them. Now problems come up, and the talented people solve them. I don't even have to get involved. It's wonderful.

In terms of advice for younger people who want to start companies like yourself—the two of us included—what are the important things to think about?

I would say to really focus on hiring great people, and learn from them. One of the challenges of a new company is that you don't really know what the right strategy is because you have to do a lot of testing and experimentation to really refine this, and get the right focus. So, experiment actively, and once you've found something that works well, elaborate on it, and focus on it.

Balance your objectives with the ability to actually achieve them. We found ourselves trying to do more things than we could do. Today, we still have significantly more opportunities than we could possibly pursue. And, we will get in a room, and we'll say, "OK, what do we want to do this year that's new and different?" And we'll come up with a list of 25 things, and we'll cross 22 things off the list, and save them for next year's discussion. Because there is no way we could possibly do them.

And does this apply in a startup as well?

The challenge in a startup is that you almost have to spread your wings pretty far to see what will work. In our case, the 25 things would all give us a ROI of more than 30 percent and are all profit-generating, low risk, good ideas. We've already weeded out the things that won't work. When you're doing a startup, you don't really know. So the faster you do the experimentation and get rid of things that don't work and keep doing things that do work, the faster you get to the winning business model.

9

CHARLES WANG

Computer Associates

Managin', New Yawk Style

C A is not a car company. Nor is it an appliance manufacturer—or an airline.

CA is Computer Associates, the second largest software
company in the world. So, why haven't you, or many other
digitheads for that matter, heard of them? Perhaps because
CA is not located in trendy Silicon Valley, but in distant dreary
Islandia, New York.

Or, perhaps because CA chiefly sells business applications:
nonsexy programs used by businesses to network computers
and crunch large numbers—programs that Joe Consumer
never heard of, or never needed. But, CA software does sell.
CA software is used by almost 100 percent of Fortune 500
companies. And with revenues of more than $3 billion, and
9,000 employees worldwide, CA has evolved from a meager
little startup into a global powerhouse.

In 1976, Charles Wang and Russ Artzt—two buddies who
met at Queens College—founded Computer Associates. Its
first major product was CA Sort, software that sorted data

faster on IBM's computers than IBM's own software. But Wang and Artzt didn't write the code for CA Sort—they acquired the rights to sell it in 1974 from a Swiss software company, also called CA. Wang sold so much of CA Sort, that he was able to buy the Swiss parent within two years.

Wang, however, isn't exactly what you'd call a smooth salesman. He is known for being abrupt, impatient, and very aggressive. Under Wang's leadership, CA has adopted a cookie monster strategy: it has acquired over sixty companies in its 20-year history. CA is also known throughout the industry for being very "objective"—i.e., brutal—about newly acquired employees. Wang and CA have laid off thousands of employees from acquired companies, and consequently have received strong criticism from the media.

Yet, in spite of his critics, Wang still impresses—not only because of what he has achieved, but also because of where he started.

Charles Wang grew up in Shanghai, China. His father was a prominent judge. But after the Communist revolution, his family fled to the United States and settled in Queens, New York. Although free, they were no longer affluent. Charles was eight years old at the time, and didn't know a word of English. And while growing up, he—like many immigrants who come to America—went through discrimination. Wang's Chinese ancestry can partially explain this.

So could his accent. Having lived on the West Coast for a couple of years, the first thing we noticed when we spoke with Charles Wang was a heavy New York accent blended with a mild Chinese twang. But, soon after we spoke about "goin' hungry" and "managin' people" and "leadin' the industry," we realized we were in the presence of a shrewd, frank New York businessman who deserves the highest accolade for his achievements.

We met with Charles Wang at CA's world headquarters in Islandia, New York.

"Managing is not just telling people what to do, but it is leading by doing."

Tell us about CA's startup process. Besides using credit cards instead of venture capital, what are the most vivid incidents in your mind?

There's nothing that really stands out in that way. It's sort of a process. Russ and I got together and wanted to do something. Every time we thought there was a better way to do something, we just started doing it.

There was no master business plan. We just lived hand to mouth. Hand to mouth. Once we had a little breathing room, then we thought about the future—but there's no future if you can't get through today.

People often ask us, "In the beginning, what was your vision?"

Our vision? Meet payroll next week. That was our big vision. We took it a week at a time. And you do whatever is necessary. That may not be the best advice to MBA students who say, "Oh my god, you didn't have a business plan?!"

No, we didn't. We just thought that we could do something different, and we could do it on our own, and we could do it better. That's it. And that's part of the beauty of not having venture capital because—

You don't have to answer to anybody but yourself.

Right.

When you first started out, you acquired the rights to sell CA Sort from the then-called Computer Associates based in Switzerland. Tell us about that process. Were you sure that this was a dynamite product that was going to sell, and if so, how did you know?

We thought through the criteria needed to allow our startup company to make and sell a major product. I really didn't want to be in consulting because, you know, they're whores—lawyers are the same way, you know. They sell their time.

I wanted to have a major product. We had some products at the time that we basically wrote for a very different operating system called VM. The problem was that the VM users were a very small community.

So we realized that we wanted something that could be used by everybody. Second, we wanted something that we didn't have to convince a user to use. I didn't want to be a missionary selling religion first and then selling my brand of bibles. Third, we wanted something that could be sold by telephone because none of us could afford to travel at the time.

So, we thought about what kind of product line would fulfill these criteria, and we landed upon system utilities. System utilities—tape libraries and disk managers—all enhance the operating system. However, most of them did things that users weren't sure if they needed or not—except for sorting. At the time, 25 percent of computing time was spent sorting, and users knew this.

There was one sorting product called CA Sort that was very successful in Europe. At the time, it was marketed by a Swiss company that didn't know anything about system utilities because they were in a market different from the system utilities market. And, we really wanted to get CA Sort.

We took a roundabout way of getting it. We first took the rights to sell another product from CA [the Swiss parent] called CA Earl which was a product that competed directly against Easytrieve, a strong software package. We knew that we'd never sell CA Earl because you just couldn't go out and compete against Easytrieve. They had a huge sales force, and we had nobody except me. So we just rewrote the manuals for CA Earl exceedingly well and packaged it really well.

And, CA in Europe was really impressed. They said, "Ah! Here is somebody who really knows how to market software products. Why don't we look at doing something with them with CA Sort?" And that's how the company started.

In retrospect, your roundabout method of acquiring CA Sort worked, but if you had to do it all over again, would you have done it that way?

That's a hard question because, you know, I don't have to do it over again.

To be honest, I don't know. There were really no choices like that. The question may be whether raising money is better or bootstrapping is better. In the software business, I think that it is better to bootstrap, because one of the problems you have when you throw money at these kids—you know, kids really—is that they have no understanding of what it is to go hungry.

They have no understanding of what it is to struggle to meet a payroll. They usually take the elegant business school approach of doing things, when really, for us, it's just great that the company was alive. Do you understand? They have no concept what it is to go hungry.

For example, we had a printroom. Sometimes on the nightshift, I went in there randomly. You would never find an MBA guy—no offense to MBAs—(*All laughed*), but you would never find an MBA guy doing that. Why? Because he's funded. That's not his job. And that's what is wrong.

So you are saying that being funded too much in the beginning affects the—

Culture—

—right from day one.

Absolutely. For example, we'd answer phones all the time even if they weren't ours. I'll go by a desk today and if the phone rings, I'll answer it. Even if it's not my desk, I'll pick it up. I'll pick it up because we still want to be small and classy—that's what made us successful.

Managing is not just telling people what to do, but it is leading by doing. That's the fun of it and people can lose that [with early funding], so if I had the choice again I would want to bootstrap.

What kind of advice can you give us on how to choose people to work on your team?

I think what you first have to do is make a list of your strengths and weaknesses. And, then, get people to complement yourself if you are going to lead.

You really have to decide what you're good at, and what you enjoy doing. Then, I'd complement myself with people that can do the things that I'm not good at and can do them well.

Part of this process is to be realistic and objective. You can't be so egomaniacal to say that you're good at everything. It's almost like athletes on a team—there are some that can play every position on the field, but you can't play them all at the same time. So you pick the best one for the team.

In CA's case, Russ is the one that I first started out with, but, financially, the person who was instrumental to get us going was my brother. He planned to stay three years in order to get us organized, get CA public, and so forth. He had no interest in software really. Thirteen years later he retired.

So you have to surround yourself with great people who complement you. Sanjay [Sanjay Kumar, the President of CA], for instance, is just incredibly bright. He's out of this world. He could run any of these companies—that's how talented he is. Sanjay does a lot of the administrative work now. But, he is also technical which gives us a great commonality—it isn't like he talks a different language than I do. He knows what it is to go hungry. He has great touch with people. So, when we look for people, we look for their best assets.

But you really need to see whether a member of your team has what I call "the CA heart." You have to believe in the company. I tell my people not to bet their career on a product or a particular job, but to bet it on the company. I try as much as possible to guarantee that we will not have layoffs, rifts, and all that because if you're betting with me, then I have to give you some kind of feeling that, "Hey, we are with you."

Right now, we are in the midst of doing a retraining of CA people because our whole foundation for the knowledge base of everything we do has shifted dramatically with the internet. We are retraining everybody in CA. It's taken over a week for every one of the people here.

Everyone through this course. Unbelievable. Most companies won't do that. Because I said now is the time to rebuild the foundation. People ask us if we are in trouble. We're not in trouble—but the time to rebuild foundations is when you don't have to. Otherwise you end up with a euphemism called reengineering.

You gave us an opening when you said that when you pick your executive team, you take stock of your strengths and weaknesses as an executive. What are yours, starting with the weaknesses?

Well, how much time do you have? (*They laughed.*)

I *hate* the administration part. I am very very poor at it. I hate the bullshit. I'm too direct, too blunt. Bob [Bob Gordon, CA's VP of Public Relations] usually has to shield me from the press at times because I say my mind.

I don't like people spinning things—don't edit it for me, just give it to me with the good and the bad. I'm a big boy. I'll take the bad news, but give it to me straight. If you start spinning it, then I can never trust you. In that sense, I'm not the best front guy and I know that. And that's a weakness.

I'm really impatient. For stock analysis and all that, Bob knows he'll use Sanjay, since he's much better at this and a little more patient. I'm so impatient it's unbelievable. I just don't put up with bullshit. By the time we argue what can and cannot be done, we would have done half of it.

Sometimes I forget my window of opportunity with a particular CA employee is very brief. He sees me for twenty minutes. I may blow his whole career by asking him, "What the hell are you doing? This is bullshit!" This poor guy goes home and cries. I blew his career. And I forget about this. So that is a weakness. I'm not the smoothest guy when it comes to being political about things, so therefore I need people around me that are better in those things.

We all have to work as a team. You really have to feed off of each other. There is no ego here, no pomposity.

For example, when we have a meeting we don't have a lot of overheads. No. We just sit down and talk about it. It's a known rule at CA that if you come to a meeting with Charles and you have a big agenda prepared, you're probably in trouble. We probably won't follow it. I know what the purpose of the meeting is and I want to go right to it. I don't need all of the background stuff. If I didn't know, then I would have asked.

And your strengths?

I enjoy working with people. I enjoy seeing people succeed at doing things. And, when somebody says to me or my team that nobody can do that, then I immediately reply, "Oh yeah? Watch us." Then we go at it. I think we enjoy that challenge of it. So, I think one of my strengths would be to look at an idea, put a team together, and then keep them working with a common vision. And make it exciting and fun and overpay them.

We have the greatest guys in the world. And we have the most fun. I have worked with so many CEOs, and I know that we have the greatest fun. There was a time when we negotiated a huge acquisition and there were two conference rooms set up. While our team was screaming and laughing, you could hear a pin drop in the other conference room. They all thought something was wrong with us, but we were just having a good time.

You've stated several times that your word is the most important thing—

It is.

Why do you feel so strongly about this, and how did this come about?

When I was younger, probably just getting to be a teenager, my father sat me in front of a mirror. He was just standing there with me, and he said, "Look at yourself." He didn't bark this out, but said it in a very mild manner. After all, he was a professor.

So, he said, "Look at yourself. What do you see?"

Being smart, I replied, "Well, I see you in there." Ha ha. (*All laugh.*)

"No. No," he said, "What do you see?"

So, I said, "I see a reflection. Not a refraction, a reflection." Ha ha ha. (*All laugh again.*)

And then he got very serious—I still remember the conversation.

He said, "Look. Just look . . . When you look at yourself, the only person there is your word. Your word is you. No matter what happens, your word—that's who you have to live with. That's the most important thing."

And that stopped me. It really made me think.

I don't need people to split hairs by saying things like, "What I meant to say was ..." *Well, if you meant to say it, say it.* If you meant to say it, then why didn't you say it?

I hate it when people start out with a preamble of conditions, "In all probability, in most cases, if everything goes well tomorrow, if the sun rises, if Mickey Mouse doesn't die, then this will happen." Come on. Just tell me it won't happen.

Don't give yourself all these nice outs. It's okay even if it does happen. But, I don't need all this bullshit, because I don't know what weight to put on it. I don't know how unsure you are when you say things like that. So, I tell people that if you give your word then keep your word. And I want it said directly. That's all.

What was the biggest test of your integrity in CA's history? Somebody who is struggling so hard to meet payroll or just get the company off the ground is at some point tested.

I don't think it's ever tested. You don't think of that. I think if you do think about that, then there is something wrong. When you give your word, you give your word, and that's all there is to it. That's it.

Even if somebody said, "But you didn't get it in writing," it doesn't matter.

For example, I was going to buy Foxpro [a database program now marketed by Microsoft] once. The guy came in here, shook hands on the deal and everything. He went back, called me up, and told me his lawyer said that since we didn't sign anything, we don't have an agreement.

So I said to him, "You're right, David. You're right. We don't have an agreement. But, you should really check with your lawyer. There is a thing called an oral contract. But, I just want you to know we don't have a deal. You're absolutely right."

If it's not signed, then we don't have a deal? Is it signed in the right place? Is that his real signature? Come on.

So you said that out of contempt.

I didn't want to work with him. When you lay down with dogs you get fleas.

Let's talk about acquisitions. CA has a reputation of being somewhat brutal in terms of its acquisitions in the sense that people are axed pretty mercilessly. Do you have anything to say about that?

Well I have a lot to say about that.

First, you have to understand that the whole strategy of CA is about internal development, acquisition, and integration. Press people get more glamour out of the acquisition piece because it has human interest. Nobody cares about integration.

With acquisitions, you have human issues, so everybody seems to focus solely on this piece. But it is really a three-piece strategy. Without one of the three, we're dead. We can't do it.

From a PR point of view, there are obviously better ways to do acquisitions. My PR people beat the shit out of me about how I do acquisitions wrong. But to me, CA has developed the bible on how to do acquisitions.

Realize that of 60-some companies that we have acquired, about 50 came to us because they were on the verge of bankruptcy—they were going under. They had to do drastic things. My own personal belief is that when I acquire a company, I owe it to every employee to tell them where they stand within one or two days, and one week at the latest. Do you have a career here—yes or no?

If you *do* have a career, then you're like any other CA employee. That's it. If you *don't* have a career here, then severance plans have to be worked out. And if you're a transition play [an employee whose status CA is undecided on], then you get a 25 percent bonus for the period that you stay, and during that time we try to look for a position for you within CA. I tell everybody that.

Do I need two marketing departments? Probably not. Do I need two accounting departments? Absolutely not. Do I need two legal departments? Absolutely not. We keep the core technical people. Sales people—whoever wants them gets them, we don't care. Throw them a little something and they run. But we keep most of the technical, support, and development people.

The time during an acquisition is of course the worst time to tell the acquired company's employees where they stand because of the instability—they're going to be acquired and they know that. They're in trouble. When you go in there all you really want to do as the acquirer is to be loved. This is the time when you want to come across as the white knight. Da-dum-da-dum-dum-dum... (*They laughed*), and what do you do?

You tell them the truth. So you get all the bad press. We get killed because all the people who get cut pick up the phone and call the press. They don't realize what they are doing to their fellow guys who are staying.

So, my PR guy says, "Why don't you do what any other company does and keep everybody?" Well, if I needed everybody, I would tell them and they would stay. I don't have a problem with that. We've acquired companies in Europe where we don't have an office and everybody stayed. They ask, "Well, why don't we do what Legent did? When Legent first merged with another company, they had two headquarters. So, we'll have two headquarters."

Horseshit. You don't have two headquarters. Then Legent acquired another company, and then they had three headquarters. Three HR departments. Three legal departments. So, why did you acquire them in the first place? What, are you the K-Mart of software? (*They laughed again.*)

I don't think it's right for us to invest in an employee when we know there's no future for him at CA. And I don't think it's right for them to be investing in a career with no future. So I tell them right away. Yeah, we could stretch it out and do six months or nine, but then think of what happens. The whole fabric and culture of CA would be torn. All the employees would be waiting for that second cutoff.

And once you start that spiral—just look at IBM. Everybody was spending their time looking at what the new severance plan was. "Do I have this in my 401(k)? Am I vested?" So we took the hard line that everybody would immediately know where they stand, and we get killed in the press for it. But, if you are going to acquire something, there must be a reason why you're doing it. And if it's really synergistic when everybody stays, then I have no problem with that.

Many acquisitions have failed and oftentimes people chalk it up to cultural differences. And it seems like you're taking care of that right from the start and just eliminating the culture difference.

Yep. There are no culture differences. There's only one culture: CA's. Period.

And people there ask us how we're going to blend the two cultures. I'm not blending any cultures. I'm acquiring you, I think. Look at your paycheck next month. I'll bet it says CA at the top left corner.

It's very hard being acquired. So, during a big meeting of the acquired company, I always tell its employees, "I want you to go home and I want you to quit. In your mind, I want you to mentally quit. Then calm down, and start a new job with CA," because if you don't say that, then you'll waste all your time with complaints like, "Our company's benefit plan had this, and CA's doesn't."

So let's say Joe Employee works at UCELE. How do you determine what to do with Joe Employee? Do you look at his résumé? Do you look at where he is in the team? What are the steps?

Okay, here's how we do it. We basically work with their present managers, and have them rank their people—

Upper level managers?

Yeah. Upper level—anybody who has ten or more people that report to them. So, we ranked his group—

According to ability?

No. Not according to ability—according to a simple criterion. We ask the manager, "If you were starting your group today, who would be the first person you hire? If I asked you to downsize your group today, who would be the first guy you let go?"

And if you have ten departments like this and they all have ten people, you now have a much better overall picture of the company. Then, I take the organizational charts from two or three years and lay them on the table. And, when we look at them and then you see who is being laterally positioned—parked—you know, you'll see positions called assistant specialist, assistant to this, special assistant to this, special consultant, etc. When you see that, chances are that you know this guy does something wrong—you'd better look closely at him.

And I then have my people interview everybody.

Everybody?

Everybody. This is what we call a "headcheck." Because they're going to be as good as they really are at that interview. We take fifteen to twenty minutes and just sit down and talk. And you get a gut feel for the guy. If something is wrong—we'll have a much better chance of knowing.

Who does the interviews?

We have senior managers here in CA that have a lot of experience and have done this before.

How do you do all of this within one or two days?

We just whoosh it through—we've done it before. We just set up the office, set up the interview and the whole system is computerized— all the rankings, everything. Then we build what CA needs. We have a pretty good feel. And, most companies that we acquire are really bloated.

One of the things you complain about in Techno Vision *[a book about technology that Wang has written] is about account control—that is, large companies such as IBM force their customers to become dependent on them. Is CA guilty of that with its customers in any way?*

Absolutely. We have to be and we should be and we hope to do that successfully. The only difference is that our account control is not biased toward a specific platform—except CA's. If you want, you can use HP, IBM, Solaris, or Windows—it doesn't matter.

There's no question about our goal for account control. But, ultimately all of this account control depends upon whether you can deliver or not. We deliver. Unicenter is *there*. The others ain't. There comes a point where you have to deliver what you say. That's the difference.

Every one of these companies is fighting for account control and we are too. Microsoft is too. Bill [Gates] thinks that everybody in the world is going to go to Windows. I think that they might, but probably not in our lifetime. He thinks that it'll be in his lifetime. I just wish he was older than me. (*They laughed.*)

You were once asked by a television reporter about making it. And you spoke about an incident in a restaurant. Tell us about that.

Well, the reporter asked me at what point I realized that I made it. And the first thing that popped into my mind was a moment in a restaurant. When you're younger and struggling, you have to watch what you spend—I still remember deciding when I was younger, whether I should have soup or have the appetizer. I couldn't afford both.

And I remember that there was a point when I was in a restaurant and I said to myself, "Shoot. I don't need to decide anymore whether to have soup or to have an appetizer. I don't care." And that was the moment. So, if that's a criteria for making it, then fine.

Is that one of your criteria for making it?

Well, what do you mean by "making it"?

What do you mean by making it?

Well, I think you never make it in a sense. You should always have a certain amount of insecurity in what you do. At this point, I'm having the greatest time of my life. My criteria of making it is to do what I want, to play with my dearest friends.

We're on a team that is just unbeatable. We have the greatest time, we laugh, we sing, we do everything together. I have the greatest people around me. The same fun is here now as it was in the beginning—so I made it. I'm still making it in that sense.

Someone as driven as you to succeed has to put a lot into your professional life. Has that ever come into conflict with balancing your personal life?

No. My personal life basically is very important. There are two sides of your life: your personal and your business. I tell all my people that when sometimes there is a crisis in your personal life, you have to just let go of the business for a while and take care of those things. It may mean your kid's sick, so you have to stay home. It doesn't matter.

There are times when you're going to have to stay really late because we have to get a project done. So, you have to balance the two. I cannot tell my people, especially my creative development group, to just turn their brains off.

But, I love my family. I spend a lot of time with them whenever I can. I travel and take them with me so that I have that time. I raised my first kid by myself. Not many men have had the opportunity to raise their own little girl. So, I know what it means to balance.

There are a lot of companies, especially in Silicon Valley, whose employees are just working all the time. Do you have any advice for managers of such companies?

I only can tell them what works for me may not be the right thing for you. But, I do go downstairs to our development area. And let's say it's 8:00 P.M., and I happen to be here late. I will abruptly walk up to a terminal where somebody is working, hit the off button, and say, "Good night!"

And then I'll walk up to the next terminal, hit the off button, and say "Good night! Hope you saved it!" (*laughter*) And I will go right down the row and just send them home. There are times when I know how hard people have worked on a project and I know they are just killing themselves. So, the following week, I'll tell them, "I don't want to see your face on Wednesday, Thursday, Friday, Saturday, and Sunday." I don't want to see you in this office.

So balance is key, and I teach my managers this all the time. I'll give you a little free advice, guys: when you have kids, you get what you pay for. Spend time with them—they grow up so fast.

I was the speaker at someone's retirement party, and I asked him why he was leaving. He said, "My son came to me last year and wanted to borrow the keys to the car. I didn't even know he drove. Then it hit me." So let me give you some advice. Spend time with your kids.

Ultimately, you see, it's not about the money we make, it's about the journey we take. You really want to make sure the journey is fulfilling. Money is one of the pieces that measures how well you did and gives you more options, but you better enjoy this journey. Don't sell yourself out just for the money piece.

I tell my people this all the time. If you want to go to another company because they are offering you more money, then go, but you're not going to be happy. But, if they are offering you better opportunities, then I have failed somehow, and let's figure it out, and if we can't, well then good luck to you and all the best.

And, ultimately you'd better be happy and have fun doing what you're doing. Otherwise, the journey sucks.

You are going to edit this, right? (*Everyone laughed.*)

Part of that fun comes from the "extras" that CA does for its employees such as having a day care center for children, or giving free breakfast to employees. How soon in a company's life should it start implementing such "extras"?

We did when we started. We didn't have day care, but we gave them breakfast. I used to play ball with all the guys. That's how we started. It wasn't to get the people. We just happened to enjoy each others' company.

The day care was just something that I really wanted to do ten to twelve years before we moved to this building. But my lawyers in the company kept warning me about liability issues. So when we finally set up this place, I told the architect to set up the day care.

And, my lawyer immediately told me that I couldn't have it. So I told him that he just didn't understand. We're having the day care, and it's your job to protect me. I'm not asking you for permission. I'm just going to do it. There is nothing illegal about it and I'm going to do it.

If I can set up an atmosphere where I can take away yet another worry from employees who are parents, then they are going to be better. That's all.

The story you told us about going in and turning off employee terminals so they stop working. Is that any indication that it's hard to give you feedback and it's hard for other employees to push back on you?

Oh, I wish it were tough. We are very open. You don't need appointments to see me. Everybody storms up here. So it's not a big deal. I also don't think it's tough, because employees recognize that when you're tough with me, I respect and appreciate you more.

If people keep telling me what I want to hear, then I tell them, "If you and I agree all the time, then one of us is redundant—and it ain't me. Now, you figure that one out." And they understand.

You said that the journey is really important. What about the journey motivates you?

If I can have an impact and do something to leave this world a little bit better, and I can get paid well for it, then I'm going to have the time of my life.

There is nothing macho about this. There is nothing here about achieving this or that or being the biggest software company in the world. People have said that at one point we were the biggest software company, but now Microsoft has passed us up.

Yeah? Big deal.

We never said we had to be the biggest. I want to be the best that we can be, though. I want us to be the best software company that takes care of its clients, takes care of its employees, takes care of its shareholders, and has a great time doing it.

If I can manage all of those things, we'll do fine.

10

BILL GATES

Microsoft

RUNNING THE PANZER DIVISION

Had you invested 10,000 dollars in a Seattle software company with the newly branded stock ticker symbol MSFT at the time it went public and had you managed to keep that stake, your stock would have at least been worth over $1 million in 1996. A cool ten-thousand percent return on your investment.

If you had been lucky enough to start the company with your own money, your net worth might exceed $20 billion. An even cooler return.

Just who is Bill Gates?

On the surface, we all know a number of facts. He is the world's richest person. His company's operating system software runs 90 percent of all personal computers. So powerful is his company that in 1995 his firm was investigated by the United States government for alleged antitrust violations.

Yet, at the end of the day Bill Gates is a businessman with real responsibilities: selling software, charting product strategy, keeping almost 20,000 people employed and meeting shareholders' now very high expectations. Along the way he has built a company comprised of many smart, talented, and aggressive people who aim to dominate practically every market they set their sights on. Whatever the management technique, philosophy, or gestalt Gates uses, it works.

Getting underneath and studying this approach was our focus when we met with this truly self-made man; anyone who drops out of college at age 19 to start a company in Albuquerque, New Mexico, and turns it into an 8 billion-dollar software company is doing something right. Just what is it?

One telling characteristic is Gates' penchant for reading biographies of the great minds of the modern era: Napoleon and Alfred Sloan of General Motors, among others. It's not surprising that Gates reads these with the premise that perhaps one of the best ways to become a leader is to understand how others did it themselves.

When Gates and his partner, Paul Allen, decided to form a company called "Micro-Soft," Allen pushed for the nascent company to produce both the computer and the software that ran on it. After all, just about everyone else was doing it. The conventional wisdom was that by locking customers in to both technologies, the provider of that computer system could lock in its customer base. Of the dozens of companies with this vision of computing, only a handful remain. The majority of today's successful companies focused on either hardware or software, did it right, and beat the rest. Microsoft was one of these companies. For several years, though, Gates, Allen, and company labored in the shadows of high-flying entrepreneurs like Steve Jobs of Apple Computer and Adam Osborne of Osborne Computer who seemingly overnight built their businesses into multi-million- or multi-billion-dollar enterprises.

Microsoft was put in business—and nearly taken out—by Ed Roberts of MITS. After convincing Gates that they were the team to write the operating system for MITS' computer, Altair, Paul Allen convinced Roberts that they could pull it off. Needless to say, sales of the Altair computer rocketed once people used this software to make the computer perform rudimentary tasks. In what was to set the standard for licensing software, Gates wrote the initial contract that gave MITS the rights to incorporate this software into its machine but left the right to distribute the software to other companies firmly in the hands of Microsoft. This licensing model dominates the industry today.

Microsoft's licensing of BASIC to rival firms angered Roberts and his corporate parent Pertec. Roberts obtained a restraining order on Gates' firm to keep them from earning revenues from their core product. Though an arbitrator ruled wholly in Microsoft's favor, Gates was fortunate not to have lost the company. Microsoft's cash hoard helped it weather what was certainly a seminal moment in the company's history.

In those early years Microsoft wrote software like FORTRAN and COBOL for just about every computer platform then on the market. Most failed. Who today remembers products like Quick Pascal, SoftCard, or even recent debacles like Microsoft Bob? Nonetheless, in an industry where up to 90 percent of startups flop in the first five years, Microsoft has a league-leading batting average.

Several perils await the startup founder whose company achieves liftoff. One is that the founder, sensing genius, decides that s/he is quite capable of handling that "vision and management thing." Another is concluding that the company needs professional management from a Fortune 500 executive only to see the seasoned manager tank the company. Bill Gates avoided both of these. In 1982, recognizing that Microsoft's internal controls were in shambles, Gates looked outside the company for someone with solid management experience to straighten out business processes. He hired Jim Towne from an Oregon firm, Tektronix, to do the job. In less than a year Gates dismissed him and reinstated himself as president before venturing outside again to hire Jon Shirley, a former Tandy executive who would go on to help lead Microsoft into the Fortune 500 over the course of his seven-year tenure.

For some entrepreneurs, achieving financial liquidity and security in the stock market is the siren's call. Today companies with meager revenues and nonexistent profits belly up and drink their fill from the public markets. Flush with cash and investor goodwill, these startups lose some of their hunger to survive and squander their advantages to fast-approaching competitors. In contrast, Microsoft waited for over ten years after going into business and racked up $140 million in yearly revenues before going public. Gates knew perhaps better than all others that past was but prologue.

In what was to be Microsoft's most challenging product development effort to date, Gates laid plans for a next-generation operating system. It would have to have the powerful graphically-based desktop metaphor of the Macintosh yet leverage the huge installed base of IBM-compatible systems running Microsoft's workhorse operating system known as DOS. There is much disagreement over how Microsoft obtained the right to develop this system that resembled Apple's, but one thing is clear: The scope of the project itself almost broke the will of everyone including Gates before it finally hit the market almost two years late in 1985.

Gates' work ethic is as impressive as his intellect. The stories of him falling asleep—at his terminal, waking up sometime later and immediately continuing where he left off—are legendary. Working in such a sleep-deprived state for several years is usually a CEO's ticket to a coronary. Perhaps it was Gates' youth that saved him from this fate. We were eager to see if he had moderated his pace and, if so, if it implied any softening of that competitive instinct.

Everyone likes the underdog and Microsoft hasn't been one for some time. New technologies for navigating the World Wide Web are the hottest things on the market since the advent of PCs. The premise is simple: any computer that is able to connect to any other one in the world has access to unimaginable quantities of information. As a new generation of startups races ahead, pundits crow that these new internet technologies lessen the need for a computer operating system, such as Microsoft's.

The excitement surrounding the internet leaves Gates & Company as vulnerable as it was when it was a ten-person outfit on the eighth floor of Two Park Central Tower in

Albuquerque. He must critically evaluate over 200 Microsoft technologies though he hasn't written code for years. And he must somehow keep Microsoft from becoming the clumsy and lumbering behemoth of the computer industry—something Microsoft employees delighted in accusing IBM of by donning t-shirts that jeered, "IBM: Weak as kittens, smart as a sack of hammers."

When we met with Gates, he had just come off a series of bad interviews. His rivals in Silicon Valley had done a good job of painting the internet as the thing to unseat Microsoft as the King of the Hill (something none of them have managed to do on their own) and the media, sensing blood, relentlessly and openly questioned Microsoft's viability. In short, we wondered if Gates might pull a Connie Chung and summarily boot us from the office after the first tough question.

"My job is the best job there is."

When Microsoft started, the conventional wisdom was to create both the computer and the software that ran on it. How did you choose to focus strictly on software?

The PC industry is about disaggregation between building hardware and building software. But there's another level in that disaggregation that's key: the hardware system versus the chips. The miracle of microprocessor technology is really what transformed computing. When Microsoft started, a computer company designed the computer, laid out the circuits, and designed the instruction sets. The chip industry today does that better than anyone else. It wasn't destined to happen, actually—DEC could have put their architecture onto a chip, and they almost did.

Today, in retrospect, things were very simple. But there were many microprocessor companies in the early days and we wrote BASIC for seven different chips. We didn't even cover all of the chips out there. It was clear that the chip companies were going to build the best chips and deliver the needed performance. If the chips were used by multiple hardware companies, then what about software? Paul and I knew how to write software. That's what we loved to do and that's what we thought we could make a contribution in: operating systems, languages, applications.

DEC didn't buy outside software. They wouldn't buy an operating system or a compiler from somebody else; it was all developed inside. So we couldn't start a company selling software to DEC or IBM. Our opportunity was a vision of a completely restructured industry where Intel did its part and we provided software to the many systems companies. Initially, we had an immense variety of customers and the taxonomy of the computer industry was much richer than it is today. The different types of computers were amazing. There were 30 word processor manufacturers and we licensed our BASIC Interpreter to 27 or 30. Now those guys are gone. The "general-purpose PC" has taken that over.

You're absolutely right, though. The insight to do a dedicated software company was key, because companies like Wang or DEC or IBM—who had lots of software expertise—didn't have that vision. They didn't treat their software skill as a key business. Of course it took a long time for the business to develop and we had many competitors, but they were all startup companies like ourselves.

So the decision to create a software-only company was based on your personal preference for software?

It's not that simple. Paul was very good with hardware and he understood it much better than I did. In fact, Paul wanted to do a hardware company. It was a great debate between us. In my senior year in high school, Paul and I both worked at TRW and the big question was whether we should start a company. Apple didn't exist at the time and MITS was still making model rockets and measurement systems. I told Paul that Intel's 8008 processor wasn't powerful enough and that we shouldn't start a company. Then the 8080 came along and it was clearly powerful. It was more powerful than DEC's PDP8 minicomputer. An amazing number of things could be done with Intel's 8080. Paul tried again: "Let's take the 8080 and make a computer with it."

Since I didn't know that much about hardware, I pushed for software. Paul eventually came around, but he went to work for MITS.

Paul and I wrote BASIC—our first product. It was almost a year-and-a-half later that we worked full-time, but the number of our early customers was just unbelievable. A lot of them went bankrupt, but most of them were companies doing a variety of different kinds of computers. For a couple of years almost half of our revenues came from Japan. Our sales approach was to say, "If you had to write the software in-house, your fixed engineering budget would be X and Microsoft's price is less than half what you dreamed you could do it for, and far better than what you could do." We competed against in-house engineering budgets. When Radio Shack made their first computer that was the question: what would the in-house costs be?

Your sales pitch was to outsource.

Yes. What Radio Shack got from us was more powerful than if they had done it themselves. But there was no notion of it as a standard. We started to promote the standard. We got people like Bob Albrecht of People's Computer Company and Adam Osborne [of Osborne Computer] to create programs on our BASIC and publish those programs. These people were famous at one time.

A variety of companies came out with applications. That's when people said, "Hey, I want Microsoft BASIC. My applications need Microsoft BASIC." That's the point when you're in a position to start commanding royalties as opposed to a fixed fee. Eventually, we knew we had enough of a brand position to use a pure royalty approach.

Let's talk about when you firmly established your market presence. Microsoft was unusual in that it waited until it had over $100 million in revenues before going public. Would you do it differently now?

Software is a very unusual business. The development work is not that capital-intensive. The first year we generated cash like mad even though we had many customers who went bankrupt—in other words, we had a wide margin for error. I always wanted to have enough money in the bank, so that if nobody paid us for a year, we'd be okay. After 1978 I was able to do that.

In 1981 we decided to do a stock option program to a very broad set of employees. In 1983 I thought, "I'll use a board of directors to get some experienced business people in here and get their advice." I created a board of directors comprised of local business leaders and one venture capitalist. The capitalists of course were very interested in Microsoft. So we spent a lot of time with them and got to know TBI [a local venture capital firm]—Dave Marquardt, in particular. It was very hands-on. We told Marquardt, "Pretend you are a board member for six months and we'll see if you really help us to hire people who can make business trade-offs." We liked that quite a bit. Dave joined the board and bought five percent of the company for a million dollars. That was their incentive to help us, but it was really business experience that they brought. The local business people didn't buy in since they weren't into venture capitalism.

We had enough stock options outstanding such that we had to start registering information. If you have a thin market for the stock, you get incredible volatility, outrageous prices. So we had to sell some shares to create some liquidity. We only went public because of the stock option plan. The money we got from going public is in the bank. That and the $23 million along with the other $5 billion currently in the bank. If I had to do it all again, I might have done a deal like UPS has done where you use a buy/sell formula and you avoid a need to go public; you keep it as a purely internal market and drive the pricing through a formula. It avoids some of the volatility and overhead that you get in the public market. Our experience hasn't been bad or anything, but in retrospect, I would choose the other route.

What are some of the pitfalls you could have avoided in the beginning?

I used to have this memo that I updated every year called The Ten Great Mistakes of Microsoft, and I would try to make them very stimulating for people to talk about lessons for the company's future. Many of our mistakes relate to markets we didn't get into as early as we should have, but the constraint was always the number of people we could hire, managing everything, and ensuring that we met all our delivery commitments—we were always on the edge. We really pushed the limits of how fast we hired people. The only real disagreement Steve Ballmer [VP of Sales and Marketing] and I ever had was when he joined the company—we had 25 people. He said, "We have to hire about 50 more people to deal with all this opportunity." I said, "No way, we can't afford it." And he said, "But that's what we've got to do." I said, "I just disagree. I'm not going to agree to that." I thought about it for a day and said, "Okay, you just hire as fast as you can, and only good people, and I'll tell you when you get ahead of the sanity picture." Here we are at 18,000 people now and still the key constraint is bringing in great people.

A couple of times we really didn't accurately assess the complexity of a project. We had a few cases where we compromised in terms of the quality of the people we hired. It doesn't really matter now, but we had some cases where we grossly underpriced our stuff; we'd bid X [for a sale] and later found out that we would have won the bid with 2X. Anyway, it's not that critical.

*When Microsoft was starting to come into its own you decided to bring
in some professional management by hiring Jim Towne as Microsoft's
first president. Why did you let him go only several months later?*

Until the day he retired, Paul Allen and I ran the company in partnership with regard to all product and technology decisions. Paul is an
incredible visionary. There would never be a Microsoft without Paul,
but as soon as Steve Ballmer came on Steve was my primary business
partner. Paul was involved in all major decisions, but in terms of
organizing and developing management, Steve and I drove that. It
was a real challenge because the demand for our capabilities exceeded what we could do. How do you decide which things to do? The
key was to never view ourselves as a service company. We had to be a
product company. We started what was called Consumer Products
Division to sell software direct to end-users. The retail channel
meant global distribution, support, manufacturing—things like that.
It was all complicated and we thought that other people must have
done it before and knew how to manage it.

We naïvely thought that there were guys who could tell us we
weren't doing things the best way. Jim Towne managed 12,000 people
at Tektronix, which made 500 different products and was 50 times
our size. We took it for granted that it was mostly a matter of convincing somebody to join our small little company. But Jim was not a
match for our environment. It was tricky because Steve and I are also
very, very close friends. Jim was in between Steve and I, so I could
never criticize Jim to Steve because I wanted things to work out. Eight
months later Jim wasn't even using his PC—it just wasn't a match at
all.

We then hired Jon Shirley, who was exactly what we had in mind.
Exactly. Jon knew a lot of things and was very helpful as we grew. He
loved the business. He was very hands-on. He was part of the team.
You can say Jon and Steve and I ran the business and all three of us
loved working together.

*Your company has a reputation for aggressively pursuing opportunity.
One Microsoft employee we spoke with said that the driving force here
is to win, win, win. Now that the company has grown so large, how do
you maintain the intensity?*

I think win, win, win is bad. I wouldn't use that phrase. I never used
that phrase with the employees. You don't ever win, you do better

products. At Microsoft we hold up competitors as an example of what we need to do. We do that well because we think of ourselves as underdogs and take a very long-term approach. We bring in great people. Those are our keys to success. You never win. We know that we have to deliver enterprise solutions better than IBM can, databases better than Oracle, machines more powerful than the one Sun ships. You don't get there overnight. That's a long quest. Our people can think about that. Are we making progress? How would you measure that progress? We never talk about the things we've been successful at. We always talk about the challenges ahead, but there is no finish line. We define the challenges so that the finish line recedes far into the future. You will never go to a Microsoft meeting and hear somebody say, "Let's win" or "We won" because that's got a finite scale to it.

Is that how you manage a company with 20,000 people?

Large companies are never as easy to maintain at a high level of excellence. It becomes the daily task. It's mostly about hiring great people. It's mostly about making sure you have a vision that's important. Microsoft is just designed to write great software. We are not designed to be good at other things. We only know about how to hire, how to manage, and how to globalize software products. Our approach may not apply to any other business. This is a business where you can find people who have enthusiasm for doing things well. You can create incredible feedback loops that guide what you do. We have many users who love to tell us how they do things.

You can design things such that even the developer gets a lot of user input. You can review what we weren't the best at, talk about it, and recognize what other companies, large or small, are doing well. We've created an organization that loves to write great software and has many great people who maintain those values. If we were a company trying to do other things, I don't think we would hold together. Microsoft's just designed for a very particular vision.

What could Microsoft be better in?

It's a matter of how quickly we are moving. Our success has allowed us to grow and get some incredible people for database and graphics, speech, vision—all the things that we think will be big in the future. In terms of enterprise computing, people are willing to use PC technology with our software to run their most demanding systems. We still have a ways to go on that. There is a huge business out there. I'm pretty pleased with the rate of progress, but there is just so much more to be done. You can look at the company lots of different ways:

- Innovation across the product lines;
- How we are developing and hiring people;
- Our financial results;
- Our market shares.

For any group I meet with at Microsoft, the whole meeting is about what I think they ought to be doing better—a little bit about some of the things that went well—but you just can't spend too much time on that. Take PC ownership cost as an example. It's too high today. A PC is too hard to install. We must work a lot to make sure that PC cost of ownership is low and that the PC is a great appliance. We have an immense amount to do in graphics and video and bringing a unified object approach to browsing and storing data. It's a deep problem in computer science. A deep, deep problem. We have too many stores of data today. We have file systems, message systems, directory systems, database systems, and all sorts of different software that optimizes all those things. That just isn't going to cut it. When you say to a small business, "Hey, get a server," they're not going to pick a database, a mail package, a communications package, read about them, install them, and learn about them independently. They are going to need one integrated thing that hides all those differences. In terms of getting to the market potential, it's all in front of us. The PC will be dramatically better. There will be a wallet-type device that you carry around. The way that you input into the machine will be far better. Just to achieve the vision of having a computer on every desk and in every home, there is a lot of great software yet to be written.

What could you personally be better at?

All successful companies are run by a team of people, and I've been very lucky with the other people who have come in and helped out. I like to focus on working with the product groups. That involves about a third of my time going out and meeting with customers, the majority of time meeting with product groups, and the remaining one-sixth for various things that don't fit either of those two categories. How do you manage the sales force and make sure that those measurement systems are really tracked down to the individual level and encourage the right behavior? I'll sit in meetings where Steve Ballmer talks about how he wants to do it, but that's not my expertise. How do we advertise to get these messages across? I sort of know where we are going long-term. I've got to make sure people are coming up with the messages consistent with that future. But I'm not expert in those things. Even in technology areas it's fun to learn new things; when I'm trying to find out where we are going with asynchronous transfer mode [an emerging standard for high-speed networking] we have experts who come in and talk to me about those things. I spend two weeks here just doing "think weeks" where I read all the stuff smart people have sent me. I get up to date to see how those pieces fit together. I'm a very product-oriented executive. That's how I spend my time, which means that in top management you've got people who look at it from a management point of view, a sales and marketing point of view, a financial point of view, and they become a key part of the team.

Can we move to Microsoft's next big challenge, building products for the internet? Some think that the rise of the internet minimizes the need for an operating system, like Microsoft's.

We're a software company and we think software will continue to be valuable. Anybody who says there is not an operating system is playing a word game with you. There is something inside the machine that you are working with. You can turn a browser [i.e., Netscape Navigator or Microsoft internet Explorer] into an operating system. You can turn a language run-time into an operating system, but the things that applications run on top of, the way they get their security authorization and do storage management, that's an operating system. So there will be an operating system. If you've met people who've said that Microsoft won't sell operating systems in the future, if you believe them, you should short Microsoft stock. There's an opportunity to make about $55 billion out there and you ought to put that on the front of the book. [*If the publisher agrees to it, we will.*]

It's a competitive market and I'm glad these guys like their products. Maybe they wanted to sell two copies of software to get you to buy them. I'm not here to talk about our products. If you think nobody is going to be doing word processing, I think that's another reason to short Microsoft stock—seriously. Maybe nobody is ever going to do any more word processing. Maybe this whole electronic mail thing just isn't that interesting. We will have to find out. I'm much more of an optimist than whoever it was you were talking about.

Okay, it seems that these competitors obviously have you in their sights. It doesn't help you that Microsoft has developed a reputation among Silicon Valley companies for a lack of integrity in its business dealings. Why does that perception exist?

I've never heard that. Maybe there is some Silicon Valley thing that you guys are involved in. I don't know. I've never heard any attack on our integrity.

Gordon Eubanks [CEO of Symantec] said that many of these companies are trying to do Microsoft in and would be better off focusing on improving their own products. Perhaps it's Microsoft's aggressiveness that causes them to say this.

We've done a lot of things with Gordon. Successful companies succeed because they have a long-term approach in dealing with employees and dealing with customers. People buy products because of their relationship with the company that makes them. They will only buy a piece of software if they know there are going to be new versions, customer support will come through, and the product takes you in the direction you want to go. It's all about the reputation that company has.

In terms of hiring great people, how do we hire all these people? It's by word of mouth. People say it's great to work here. The stock value has a huge impact on employees, customers, stock holders, everybody, and reflects the long-term approach and strength in the company. We've never had any dispute about anything because we just move forward. The question takes me aback, really.

What's aggressive? Shipping a good product. That's aggressive. Lowering the price of the product so more people can get it. That's aggressive. Those are good things. We're here making good products, taking all the phone calls, meeting with the users, hiring smart people. That's all our business is.

With IBM, we both benefited immensely from that relationship, and we still have a lot of positive relationships. They're our second biggest customer after Compaq. They decided not to work with us on operating systems and to go down their own path. That certainly wasn't our choice. They even got to keep the old name of the product we produced jointly.

You've certainly shipped a lot of product. When do you think Microsoft's incredible growth will plateau?

We've always said that, given our long-term approach, this business will definitely go through cycles. There will be ups and downs. There haven't been yet, but we are still sincere about saying that. We say our profitability, percentage-wise, has grown at an unsustainable rate. We are clear about that. However, if you take the right perspective, there is a lot of value in lower cost communications and lower cost computing. It simply means that great software will be more valuable. The only question is how we maintain leadership in delivering software. We certainly feel very good about our ability to do that. We will never grow at the percentages that we did in our early years. That's just not possible. Ask any analyst about our company, we take the most conservative perspective of any company that you'll find. We are always telling analysts, "Don't recommend our stock. We sell software, not stock. Lower your earnings estimate, be more conservative." It's not a long-term approach to promote the stock in any way.

You'll soon see that we have major upgrade cycles. Our revenue will be less consistent than it was. Windows 95 is a big upgrade cycle and it will be two to three years before we get an equivalently huge upgrade cycle. We are a company with an incredible future. We are one of the most valuable companies in America and I think it reflects people's optimism about the people here and what software can be.

Microsoft's stock appreciation has been lucrative for Microsoft employees. Will you have employee retention and recruitment problems if earnings growth slips?

People who have worked at companies that failed have a lot of good experience in thinking through the trade-offs. Many of the managers we hire have that background. I've talked about how success is a lousy teacher. We set up big challenges and we set high goals. People don't always meet those goals. It's an environment where we discuss the mistakes we've made and this company has had a chance to make lots and lots of mistakes. Our people have learned from many projects. They've seen both the positive and negative aspects. Sure, as companies go through tough times you find out who has the wherewithal to solve problems and take the right approach. It's a good thing for companies. I look forward to it. There is nothing imminent for us, though.

In the beginning you worked a tremendous amount. Is it less now?

I work long hours, but not as long as I used to and certainly haven't expected other people to work as hard as I did. My job is the best job there is and I get a lot of variety. I travel around and see customers. I see such a variety of the product groups that it's very stimulating. I work long hours.

Twelve to fifteen hours a day?

No. It's a rare day when I'll work more. There are days that I work fourteen hours, but most days I don't work more than twelve hours. On weekends I rarely work more than eight hours. There are weekends I take off and I take vacations.

In the beginning the company totally depended on you. Even now it seems like it's dependent on you.

Not really. The company has five billion dollars in the bank.

But that alone is not enough.

Enough for what?

Enough to sustain growth and momentum. Is the structure in place to compensate if you left Microsoft today?

We'd have to see. They'd have to pick somebody else to run the company. Who knows? The guy could do a better job. A CEO transition is probably a very risky transition for a company. I'm a younger CEO than you'll find in most companies and more committed to my job than most. Nobody is going to get me interested in some other job or activity, so it's very unlikely that we'd face that challenge, but it would be a challenge to the company in terms of picking new leadership. Who knows how the new CEO would do?

There are an immense number of good people here. The whole notion in the press of personifying a company through one person or very few people is a gross simplification, and it totally misstates the picture.

Think of whatever your favorite Microsoft product is. The people who created that product did it without too much coding or design work on my part. I helped create a system that allows people to manage their own products. They understand how to manage those products very, very well. That's the company's real asset.

How is your role as CEO different today from your role in Microsoft's early days?

The key to starting out was having the right code, but eventually I had to sell the software, write contracts, and learn how to hire people and make sure their code was pretty good. It's quite a contrast to what I do today. Today I don't write code. None of the people who work directly for me write code, though there are few who have. If you go from the beginning to the end, it's quite a change, but it's been gradual and I enjoy it. It's something to learn and figure out how to do well. That's a big difference between myself and a lot of people who fade away. They just aren't as interested in what the next stage requires and fitting into the role it requires. In terms of starting a company and running it 21 years later, it's surprising that it's not more common. I think it has to do either with people's adjustment to success—there are always distractions there—or their enjoyment with the new imperative tasks of a CEO.

What would you tell entrepreneurs starting companies today?

We didn't start Microsoft with any notion of it becoming a large company. Our vision implied it would be a large company, but we were pretty humble about taking it one step at a time. We picked the field to go into because we enjoyed it and were excited to contribute. In the world of technology there is room not only for a few big, big successes, but for thousands of wonderful companies that are successful along all the appropriate matrices: innovation, developing great people, having good common sense, and economics that make it all work.

I've always rejected the term "entrepreneur" because it implies that you're an entrepreneur first and a software creator second. I didn't say, "Oh, I'll start a company. What will it be? Cookies? Bread? Software?" No. I'm a software engineer and I decided to gather a team together. The team grew over time, built more and more software products, and did whatever was needed to drive that forward. Entrepreneurship to me is an abstract notion. I don't think that most people who are really into their entrepreneurship aren't going very far. Seriously. Maybe I could be wrong. I wonder if the people in this book think of themselves as entrepreneurs. I don't think they do.

Those who have been in the business for a long time seem to dislike the term.

Yes. There may be some reason for that. If "entrepreneur" means people who love businesses, this group fits. But if it means people who said, "I'm going to be excited every day because I'm going to be like one of these big businesses," it just doesn't work. You've got to enjoy what you do each day for itself and for its excellence. Sure, you can take a long-term perspective to how you manage technology, employees, and customers and if your vision is sound, those long-term approaches will pay off. You'll achieve the appropriate size, whatever your vision is. Many people take a modest-sized vision and try to turn it into something larger than it can naturally be. That's very difficult. Or, they read books about how it's all about winning and they think about how tough they are going to be. But it's nice to just ship good products. I don't care how tough you are, it's kind of meaningless. Articles love to play on toughness or competitiveness, or slogans, or things like that. Software is about millions of details. You've got to have people that love dealing with those kinds of details and then taking feedback. That's what makes it a fun business.

What aspect of the computer industry would you recommend starting in today? It's hard to start a company today that develops PC operating systems.

There are people who have done it. Netscape's basic view is to take a browser and turn it into an operating system. There are many people going after that. It's a swinging-for-the-fences kind of approach. At any one time there are a finite number of operating systems that are very successful. Some people will accomplish it and many people will take a more content-oriented or a vertical industry type of approach.

If you really want to write great software, the best thing is to go work with a group of people who are very good and work on a variety of different products. If you really want to be a great software developer, you need a lot of seasoning. Thinking that you will be one of the world's greatest software developers without working alongside someone with seniority...I doubt that's a very craft-oriented view.

So if you were starting out today you would take a scatter-shot approach to developing products?

The notion of what to do at a different point of time is hard to say. I almost decided to go into mathematics. I thought I was going to go into physiological psychology. Economics? They haven't figured out much there, that would be cool. And yet my whole life I've played around with software. In math, I realized "Hey, this is not a field with a lot of virgin territory—a field with great psychic rewards for the progress you make," whereas with software it's "Wait a minute, we can do ten times better than the stuff that's been done." The opportunity and the vision that grew up around personal computing and being able to hire friends all came together. If you want to be a great software developer, go where the great software developers are. I had done a lot of work after the age of 13 studying microsoftware and I became a fantastic developer, but I kept asking great developers to look at my code and show me where it could be better, how it could be different. I'd move to a new level. When Microsoft started, there was a lot of camaraderie of challenging each other: "Can you tighten up this code? Can you make this better?" It was an era of great craftsmanship. It was a different world.

There were a lot of paths I could have taken and been pretty darn happy with.

11

ANDY GROVE

Intel

AN IMMIGRANT IN THE TRENCHES

On Tuesday morning at 8 A.M., roughly 120 glazed eyes were focused with laserlike concentration on a Stanford business school professor as he entered our classroom. It was the beginning of my second year in business school, and, in this particular class, our professor was Andy Grove, the Chairman and CEO of Intel, a multi-billion-dollar organization and one of the largest companies in the world. The B-school rumormill diligently had spread gossip about Grove—about his tenacity, distaste for tardiness, his spartan discipline—and many of us were both excited and intimidated by the prospect of being taught by him.

While I must admit that I am still slightly daunted by him—perhaps because of his remarkable achievements—Andy Grove is really a down-to-earth person and very approachable. He and Bill Hewlett were indeed this book's "bell cows"—once other CEOs knew that Grove and Hewlett were participating in *Giants*, it suddenly became surprisingly easy to land interviews with them.

The immigrant son of a Hungarian dairyman, Andras Grof was born in Budapest, Hungary, in 1936. In school he dabbled in opera and journalism. After the 1956 Soviet invasion of Hungary and subsequent "nationalization" of his father's business, Grove escaped on a boat filled with refugees, and landed in New York with only $20 in his pocket. Three years after landing on U.S. soil, Grove graduated first in his class from the City College of New York with a degree in chemical engineering, paying his way through college by being a waiter. Three years later, he obtained a Ph.D. from UC Berkeley and used his writing skills to craft *Physics and Technology of Semiconductor Devices*—considered even today to be the seminal introduction to semiconductor engineering for students.

Grove left Berkeley to work for Gordon Moore and Robert Noyce, founders of one of the world's first semiconductor companies—Fairchild Camera and Instrument, later named Fairchild Semiconductor. After being dissatisfied with Fairchild's progress, Noyce and Moore went on to found Intel (INTegrated ELectronics) and brought Grove with them to head the R&D department. After a stint in R&D at Intel, Grove became COO in 1976. In 1979, he launched Operation Crush, a campaign to capture 2,000 new customers away from Motorola within one year. Intel beat that goal by 500 customers, one of which was IBM.

In 1982, IBM approached Intel to provide its 8088 microprocessor chip as the brain of IBM's entry into the microcomputer industry—the IBM PC. Ironically, Intel had already developed and patented the microprocessor in 1971, but did not expect significant demand for it.

However, in 1985 personal computers weren't shipping in enough volume. Intel had defined itself as "*the* memory company," yet its memory business evaporated. The Japanese chipmakers had driven prices so low that they crushed their U.S. rivals in the huge market Intel had invented. Intel, the industry leader, lost money for six straight quarters from the withering attack of Japanese firms, and many in the industry doubted Intel's ability to survive. Over the objection of several executives, Grove axed the DRAM business and thousands of employees. Unwilling to let the company come to such a pass again, Grove focused Intel on microprocessors with a paranoia and manic competitiveness that set the culture for the company today. Indeed, Intel's overarching theme of "Only the Paranoid Survive" (also the title of one of Grove's books) epitomizes the current Intel culture.

Intel's revenues grew as the personal computer industry mushroomed. Its microprocessor design quickly became the *de facto* industry standard for the bevy of new computer and software developers just starting up. Nowadays, the words "Intel Inside" are the words by which many Americans judge the quality of the computers they buy, resulting in about a whopping 80 percent market share for Intel.

Yet, despite the fact that the company's stranglehold on the microprocessor market shows no sign of loosening, Grove has not rested on his laurels. Intel spends a significant amount of its revenue on R&D, and consistent with his paranoia, Grove still considers the industry and his competitors to be brutal. Intel and its competitors—most notably Advanced Micro Devices, or AMD—often take their battles to court using hardball legal tactics. Grove has referred to AMD as "the Milli Vanilli of semiconductors. Their last original idea was to copy Intel. Since they can't win in the marketplace, they try to defeat us in the courts and press." Yet, polemics aside, Intel has managed to keep its smaller competitors from undercutting the company's business. AMD has always hovered around 10 percent of the microprocessor market.

Despite the furious competition, Grove manages to teach high-tech strategic management at Stanford's business school, and also is a prolific writer. He is the author of three management books: *High Output Management, One-on-One with Andy Grove*, and *Only the Paranoid Survive*.

We had breakfast with Andy Grove at Hobee's, a popular restaurant in Mountain View, California.

"The important things of tomorrow are probably going to be things that are overlooked today."

What do you think your talents are as an entrepreneur and as a manager of a large company?

One thing is important for me to correct: I never looked at myself as an entrepreneur, and even today I don't look at myself as an entrepreneur. In Intel's case, the entrepreneurs were Bob Noyce and Gordon Moore. Gordon himself is a little uncomfortable with the word "entrepreneur." In speeches he'd describe himself as the accidental entrepreneur.

Now, that's not the case for Bob. Bob's really more of an entrepreneur. But, I just tagged along for the ride. That changed later. Much later. But in the early stages my expectations were that I'd be head of R&D for this new company. R&D is what I did at Fairchild. I never pictured myself doing anything substantially different. But, I rapidly veered away from that ambition when I became the operations guy inside Intel. That's what I did for almost twenty years. I helped make Intel's transition from an entrepreneurial outfit, none of which was my doing, to the manager of a medium-sized company, which was actually a very difficult transition to make.

Why was it difficult?

Well, everybody can start a startup and come out with one product—you see that all over. But, making the company into something of a self-sustaining institution, with its own methods and mores and organization—that's tough. Transitioning people from a completely task-oriented mentality to more of a process-oriented mentality, particularly since those people were attracted to a startup, was very hard.

So, I wasn't comfortable with the role of the entrepreneur as you define it—somebody who starts a business and sees a business opportunity. I was not even qualified for that. I was a researcher. But once I began to see the architecture for the company as an organization, I became more of a participant.

So if Robert Noyce hadn't left Fairchild then you wouldn't have gone?

The person I followed was Gordon. I worked with Gordon at Fairchild and actually, I wasn't that enamored by Bob [Noyce] at Fairchild. I knew him, he was two levels above me. I got to know him better later, but at Fairchild I saw his weakness. Fairchild was a troubled organization and Bob was not comfortable running a controversial, troubled company, so he became passive as the company was spinning out of control. So I didn't have high regard for him at that time. As Gordon was leaving, I immediately volunteered to go with him. Then, I found out that Bob was leaving, and I had momentary second thoughts. That's not the conventional wisdom because Bob was very highly regarded.

You've mentioned that Intel was a collection of strangers working together, and that made things difficult in the beginning. In retrospect, do you think there were pitfalls there that you could have avoided in that respect?

No. There are pitfalls there, but I don't know how you can avoid them. First of all, the fallout didn't depend on whether we were or weren't strangers. That attitude went away after a while. What made it difficult was *not* that we didn't know each other—what made it difficult was that we didn't have any rules. Nobody quite knew what to do. Then, a lot of the people—including quite possibly myself—started developing a pecking order. Influencing and elbowing gets so illogical, and so inappropriate for a group of people who are trying to get something going. In fact, I think that there was more politicing and game playing at Intel in its first year—at least in senior management—than since its history afterwards. It's not what you would think.

How, then, does one turn political shenanigans into cohesiveness? Is it something that just happens as a matter of course or do you try to mold the culture?

[*Long pause*] It's hard to answer that without getting awfully personal. I don't have a big theoretical model or some five-forces diagram here. What I can say is that in the fortunate companies, certain operating methods emerge. And, at Intel, some methods of influence emerged.

For example, I didn't have an easy time with our first marketing manager and I couldn't spend a lot of energy marketing. I was the operations guy at Intel. And so, what happened was that we were second guessing each other and fighting, and then we got a new marketing manager three years later. That was a major breakthrough because we got along right from the get-go. I'd have to say that there was a personality conflict that did not exist with the second guy. But, who knows? Maybe by the time the second guy came in, some shape and order to the place had emerged. Had he been there from the beginning, we still might have been ridden with conflicts. I don't know.

The problem with a lot of these stories is that they are very personal and very self-centered. I'm telling you the story from my perspective and, on top of it all, filtered through 25 years of memories. Those stories make what I did seem wonderful and what other people did, less wonderful. But all our histories are like that, I suppose.

Anyway, that particular interpersonal conflict was the most important to me, but by no means the only one. We had productive people flip out or go through a kind of burnout process. When you're 30 years old and encounter that... It's not an ideal startup situation.

What was the first critical juncture at Intel—the fork in the road that could have made you or broken you? Was it when IBM decided to use your products?

The first critical juncture was the introduction of our first successful product, the 1103—the first DRAM. It was *enormously* difficult to get it into production. DRAMs were so difficult to make and test. We were learning totally new things—a new process, a new product, new testing, new customers. And, customers were seriously relying on these things for mainframe memory. We weren't playing with calculators here. We were playing with big time memory, a very difficult period.

So, that's probably what I'd put my finger on—this process and these events when we became a company. Up until then we were a new startup just coming out with our first products, none of which were that successful. Then we made the 1103 and it became very successful. That's when Intel's systems as we know them today emerged. Had we blown that [product] we probably would have followed a completely different trajectory. We might have survived, but with the introduction of the 1103 into market, the real Intel was born.

From the get-go, did you think that the 1103 was the way to go? Was it part of a master plan at Intel?

No. We found that the 1103 was going to be a sexy product. And, in the last year of production, we had to systematize it. It was the end result that dictated the style. There was no master plan whatsoever. We were running out of money and licensed the products and technology to another Canadian company. Things were much simpler and much more haphazard in the early '70s than they are today. In the midst of this the microprocessor was born. That was not a big event, though. It was an interesting thought and nobody paid a whole lot of attention to it.

It [the microprocessor] was done in response to a customer request, right?

Yes. We obviously didn't realize how important it was.

Do you think that's true of many important technologies—that you don't realize their importance?

Probably. The important things of tomorrow are probably going to be things that are overlooked today.

The important thing to realize is that a lot of major business decisions, such as Intel's shift to microprocessors, are not that obvious. In retrospect, they might be, but not when you're looking forward. If you read the newspapers about Apple, what they are going through is very similar. Nothing is obvious about Apple—other than the fact that they are in trouble. That's very obvious, but what to do about it is not obvious. If you lined up three or four of the people in your book and gave them a blank sheet of paper that said, "If I were CEO of Apple I would...," each would have a different answer.

It was like that at Intel in 1985. You could have asked five people where the company should go and you probably would have gotten five different answers. In retrospect, we know what happened with the 386, but up until the 386, the microprocessor was really not that big. Our new product was very complex. When we threw ourselves into the microprocessor business, we didn't know if we could make it. This was 1985—before we introduced the 386. And the microprocessor business was much much less than Intel's memory business at the time. So, everything was very murky, and it wasn't an obvious decision.

You asked about when IBM adopted our product. I didn't think it was colossally important at that time. And, I maintain that nobody at Intel did.

But, here's the rewriting of history: We just had the ten-year anniversary of the PC a few years ago, and the Intel newspaper wanted to interview a bunch of people about it. All of a sudden everybody remembered what a big celebration our microprocessor was at the time it was introduced. Well, I must have been on vacation. I don't remember any celebrations. I don't remember anything like that. It was good, but keep in mind that IBM thought the lifetime production of PCs was 200,000! IBM thought that the projections were too optimistic in the first place. Why would we have been more knowledgeable about how successful IBM was going be with the PC than IBM?

So, it was not a big deal at the time. What *was* a big deal was then they came around a year later, unrelated to the PC, and wanted to buy into Intel.

And they actually did take an ownership stake.

We struggled with that, whether we should let them or not. For some reason, we turned it into an existential debate: Should we or should we not? Finally we did, and the whole thing turned out to be a non-event. They never did anything related to that investment with us and they sold our stock. It was a joke—"a long-term investment" that a few years later they sold because the stock went up and they wanted to bail-out their earnings. So it turned out to be nothing. But at the time it was, "Oh, my God!" All of a sudden I was flying to New York and was meeting with the Chairman of IBM for a big announcement. It was a big deal at the time, and yet turned out to be nothing. That was in '82.

But, the big milestone was the DRAM case [shifting from DRAMs to microprocessors]. That was the crisis that shaped the Intel of today. Just about everybody in management thought it was the end. That's where the paranoia and all that stuff came from. You can't go very far at Intel without running into people who went through it.

My father worked at Intel during that time, at the Santa Cruz plant, which was shut down.

What did he do?

I don't know. When you're young, you never know what your dad does.

I had no idea.

So, when you decided to lay off a third of the workforce, obviously that must have been difficult. How does such a decision get made?

Well, we never laid off a third of the workforce in one fell swoop. We laid them off ten percent at a time, three times. That's not what we wanted to do. I have this saying: you never cut enough soon enough. At the time, Gordon said, "Let's make sure we cut enough so we can take care of all of this in one layoff." And, I said sure.

We tried to do that. But, we had just barely finished the layoffs, and it became clear that our business had sunk some more. Nobody ever forecasts that revenues will go straight down. Everybody thinks the low point has been reached.

So, we went through excruciating detail figuring out who we needed to let go. It wasn't enough so we kept doing it until finally it was enough. The transitions that we talked about earlier made us a company: employees, organizations, doing things correctly, and doing things well. But when we had to cut people back—we did that very seriously too—from the standpoint of doing it right from the employees' standpoint. As right as you can do it. Did your father get laid off?

Yes.

Then this will be a weird conversation. The prevailing industry practice at that time was to cut back on seniority—where the most recently hired person goes first. The justification was that, unless you cut back that way, you gave unions an opportunity to come in and say, "We're going to make you guys do it right." I took a very strong exception to that. We had some layoffs in the '70s—also pretty big for a small firm—and the personnel people wanted it done in a very organized way. I really leaned towards us laying off on the basis of merit, which we didn't. We gave it lip service but it was too complicated. By the time this '85 situation came up, we went to the point where we took people's performance reviews and systematically tabulated the ratings of the performance reviews and all that stuff. We did it on the basis of measurable, documentable performance. That was the compromise. We were going to do it on the basis of performance, but it had to be objective enough, so that if somebody questioned it later, you knew you had a well-defined system. We used seniority to break the ties. We spent incredible time working on it. I remember the first layoff—it was in Oregon. I went through the list name by name by name to make sure. There were hundreds of names. Most of them I didn't know, but I wanted to make sure that we were really doing what we said we would do. We took layoffs pretty seriously.

In 1982 we had a bump in our business and everybody else was laying people off. Luckily we thought it was just going to be a blip. We turned out to be right. We decided to stop hiring and did all kinds of weird things like making people work an extra ten hours a week for the "125-percent solution." We really held expenses down and stretched our employees' days longer. Our people did that literally for six months. Then we gave them a big party. Then we had another blip and we cut pay by 10 percent. So, we tried a bunch of different means.

We were very anti-layoff, because in those days people laid off left and right. Management didn't give it a second thought. We were trying to build a solution—you can't treat your people like an expense item. We really tried [not to have layoffs], but in 1985, it got beyond that. Actually, I didn't agonize too much over the Santa Cruz plant. What I really agonized over was Barbados, an assembly plant that largely built memories. There was nothing in Barbados but us. It was a resort. You would either go fold sheets at the resort or go work at Intel. It was a very stupid thing for us to put a plant there. It was very very difficult to run, but by 1985 it was a good plant. There was no history of any industrial undertaking on the entire island of Barbados, so we had to teach everybody. We went through plant manager after plant manager until we finally got it right and the plant was good. They were so proud. It was a high profile thing.

The layoffs were a major part of our maturation as a company.

So, given the choice between hiring people and laying them off in bad times versus not hiring enough people and making them work at greater expense to the company, which would you do?

The second. I have a very strong personal dictate that we as a company not lay people off again like we did before. The memory of the incident remains.

Perhaps you'll never have to make that type of decision again because of the industry you're in. It seems like you're in a pretty nice industry. Do you ever see a downturn in the semiconductor industry?

Well, it did go down in '85. There were all kinds of arguments about the semiconductor trade agreement. We were in bad shape as an industry then. There was no PC industry to keep us up. I don't think semiconductors is a nice industry. I don't think it's a cushy industry.

It's a very tough industry. Look at the people that we compete against. You don't know the meaning of competition until you've dealt with a Samsung. We have had incredibly dedicated competitors.

So, which one of your competitors in particular concerns you the most?

Nobody in particular because competition is not the issue in our case. It's in navigating change from the fairly well-defined PC industry into the network computing industry and it's very, very complex. I think probably my biggest fear is the process of navigating into the next stage of computing. Whenever microprocessor power becomes less important than before, that means a loss of business for us, much more so than a loss of business to a competitor. Competitors are much easier, this threat is just kind of ambiguous. There exists a rising tide that controls the industry. Competitors either matter or don't matter depending on that tide.

Speaking of this tide, then, do you envision the idea of just an empty set-top box with a network connection?

No, I don't see that, but what I do see is the need to develop the type of application that uses the hidden, latent microprocessor power. At home, which is where all the talk about appliances are, the bench-mark set by television, the visualization of television is what people expect in terms of processing power. So we're going to need process-ing power, but that's only half of our business. The other half is with businesses. So we have to take the initiative on stimulating applica-tions, visually compelling applications, business applications. That's our job, but it's not about competitors.

Or, increase demand.

Right. We have to generate our own demand.

Let's switch gears a little here. Why do you teach at Stanford?

Because I enjoy it. It's very simple. I've always liked teaching. I taught both during my engineering days and then during the period of time when Intel made the transition into more systematic manage-ment. I started teaching management practices at Intel, out of which came *High Output Management.*

I like exchanges. Harvard did a case on Intel. I became aware of it, and I talked to the class. I liked that. I wasn't going to go back and forth to Harvard each year to teach the case so I approached Stanford and really liked it. It's a laboratory to try new ideas. Cases allow you to think through a particular industry much more. The process ended up being very helpful to me in understanding the interaction of the internet, the World Wide Web and the like. I didn't really learn any new facts about it, but preparing the case and going to class really helped. That's a secondary reason.

Given all of your extra-Intel activities, such as writing a management column, and teaching a course at Stanford, what kind of hours does the CEO of Intel put in? Do you work less or more than before?

It hasn't really changed over time. I spend a lot of time thinking about the industry. Our industry has an impact on every other industry. Telecommunications—I used to pay no attention whatsoever to the telecommunications industry. It has now become vitally significant. International events have become vitally significant. Now the media industry is where the telecommunications industry was a few years ago—on the fringes—it gets increasingly significant. We capture people who are in the media and going into digital technology. We capture their efforts on PCs. That's our business.

So, I have to read a third of the newspaper, even though it doesn't mention Intel or the article doesn't have anything directly to do with Intel. In that context I think a lot about the world. Not so much about Intel, per se. So what are my days like? I start at 8 o'clock, end at 7. I've got another hour of work that I do at home.

Seven days a week?

No, five days a week. And over the weekend, I have maybe three to five hours of work. Not administrative things, but really the longer things that I didn't do during the week. I don't do a lot of administrative work anymore. Craig Barrett [President of Intel] does that. I figured I'd written all the performance reviews that I needed to write and I washed my hands of all of that some years ago. I really do what I want to do, but what I want to do adds up to be more than I would like it to be. This is a problem. I will be sixty years old this year and soon I'll probably have to stop. Ten years ago, I said I would retire at age 55, and I don't want to hang on too long.

Today the semiconductor industry is not one that a young Ph.D. can get into and start a company on a hope and a dime.

Not on a dime.

Many dimes. If you were starting over today, what industry would you recommend to young people trying to start a company? Would it be in semiconductors?

First a point about startups. I can't look at a startup as an end result. A startup to me is a means to achieve an end. A lot of your business school friends come up to me and say, "Hey, Andy, I want to do a startup. I want to do an Intel. So, what should it be?"

It just doesn't work that way. Instead, you should first figure out that you want to do, say, semiconductor memory. You want to do semiconductor memory so bad that it hurts, and you can't do it where you are. So you do it within a startup. Otherwise, it's such an ass-backwards way. People who did it exactly like that saw a mountain of opportunities that weren't there.

If the question is what field would I go into as a young person today I would probably get into genetics or biotechnology. I know very little about it, but it fascinates me from the following standpoint: it is the new frontier that can use computing power and increasingly even semiconductor technology in terms of preparing and building genes. It is in converging technologies which I always liked.

I see the possibility of cross-fertilization of genetics or biotech with information technology, which is very advanced and very powerful. Computational tools are very powerful. The concepts are very powerful. Software designs are very advanced. Semiconductor technology is very advanced. I'd apply it to a field like genetics which is still very, very raw. It's kind of like the semiconductor industry was in the 1950s. So I would prefer to go there. If I had to go back to school again, I would get a double degree in computer science and genetics. I don't exactly know what I would do with that, but it would be a combination of those two subjects.

You wrote an article for the Wall Street Journal *about the importance of immigrants to this country's future. How do you think immigrants have helped Intel?*

Fifty percent of our Santa Clara technical staff is Asian. There's no question about it. The degree is not as high in the other locations, in

Oregon it is probably 20 percent. Our company is interwoven. The man who discovered EPROMs is Israeli.

It's very interesting that you mentioned the article. I wrote a regular management column. I never got responses to any of my columns. But the response to this one article was incredible—e-mail after e-mail. I had a lot of feedback. In one message I got a one liner, and in another, three pages of philosophizing.

Why?

I don't even know. Are you asking a larger question?

The political thinking in the air today. The Gingrich approach to things. Proposition 187. It has become an atmosphere of intolerance and, although it may be just a minority standpoint, this attitude seems to be more prevalent than before.

It's incredible to me that with the monumental problems that we have financially as a country, there are people who target welfare mothers. It rubs me the wrong way. It really does. I had a very positive experience as an immigrant here. Nobody has ever given me a hard time. Nobody has begrudged me anything. It's never been an issue. I've become a rabid American as a result of it. I haven't gone back to Hungary at all. I have no love lost for my origins. But I hate seeing this kind of thing developing. You know every trend in this country starts in California. I can't say that it's a major trend yet, but it's enough of a trend that California has Proposition 187. Think about it.

Is there anything you can do to change that?

Probably the most important thing I can do is to run Intel in a good way. Intel's a big community, you know. There's very little I can do outside that's going to affect a community of forty-five thousand people. You can take that number and multiply it by four for the number of people that are affected in terms of employees, families, and customers. What I do at work, in some ways, affects hundreds of thousands of people. That's pretty big.

12

TRIP HAWKINS

Electronic Arts/3DO

CREATIVITY, THE ULTIMATE GAME

By 1985 Atari was in financial ruin. ActiVision's once popular game system was passé and hundreds of developers worked in a flea market environment desperately trying to sell their games to a customer, and market, that didn't exist. Prudence would judge it a dumb place to start a video game cartridge company. Trip Hawkins did just that and clawed his way past 135 other competitors to make Electronic Arts the undisputed leader in video game software development.

By all accounts, Hawkins has for many years been both an entrepreneur and game aficionado. As a Harvard undergraduate he created a fantasy football game that nonetheless folded, and with it his father's seed capital of $5,000. Apparently unfazed, Hawkins immersed himself in the study of games, graduating with a custom degree in strategy and applied game theory. His thesis: a computer model for World War III.

Hawkins came across Mike Markkula while researching the video game market as a Stanford MBA student. Markkula, looking to build a solid team for his startup venture, Apple Computer, persuaded Hawkins to join after graduating from business school. As employee number 68, his charter was to gain entry for Apple products in the business market.

Despite Apple's commercial success, Hawkins chafed and left the company in 1982 to start up his own as soon as his $7.5 million worth of stock options vested.

Taking good measure of the imploding game industry, Hawkins set out to create a company different from the one-hit wonders that pervaded the marketplace. His company, Electronic Arts, borrowed from the Hollywood studio model of media production: project managers were called producers and software game programmers were called artists and given the tools, respect, and freedom to work as the talented, creative people they were.

A stream of successful products spewed forth. Though the market was cluttered with dozens of different hardware standards, two emerged to dominate the industry: Nintendo and Sega. Hawkins bet heavily on the latter and reaped the benefits. Electronic Arts boasts yearly revenues in excess of $600 million—a behemoth in the software game industry. Hawkins' own personal fortune has swelled to the neighborhood of $200 million.

A successful entrepreneur, a captain of industry before age 40, Hawkins might have felt content to ride his company toward comfortable revenue growth, new markets, and industry respect. But in 1993, Hawkins took the highly unusual move of appointing a successor at EA and promptly leaving to start his next venture in home computer gaming, The 3DO Company. The firm's ambitious charter was to develop its own game-playing machine and leverage the technology by licensing it to companies around the world.

Hawkins' try at a veritable double dip is complicated by the presence of several large companies including Nintendo, Sega, Sony, and Philips, not all of whom care to see Hawkins promulgate a hardware standard for the industry and capture the profits from doing so.

An excellent dealmaker, Hawkins initially enlisted support from companies like AT&T, Matsushita, Goldstar, MCA, and Time-Warner. Nonetheless, young 3DO's success is far from assured.

In the months prior to our interview, Hawkins' notoriety had extended to the popular press; *Billboard* magazine anointed him "the guru of interactivity" and, in a less scientific study, *People* magazine judged him to be one of the 50 most beautiful people in the world.

Perhaps as a backlash to the adulation, business reporters' coverage of 3DO became more aggressive, criticizing 3DO's nonexistent profits despite the company having already gone public. Some predicted imminent doom for the company.

It was at this time that we met with Hawkins at his corporate headquarters, just a stone's throw from Steve Jobs' company, NeXT, to understand the creative drive behind the biggest name in games.

"A true entrepreneur is a creative person, who doesn't do things to make money—he does them because he has no alternative."

How important is it to have a completely original idea in order to start a business?

I guess there are two ways to look at businesses: you can start one that is based on a big, new idea or you simply start one that works on an established idea. But even if it is something like starting a restaurant—obviously, there are other restaurants—the big idea may be why your restaurant is different from the rest. Yours may have a completely different approach to some common aspect of the business.

But there is nothing novel about starting a restaurant.

Exactly. One unseen aspect of business is that we all know about the success stories but never hear about the failures. I know what the batting averages look like in my industry because I've seen the turnover of companies for a long period of time. These batting averages are pretty poor. Some of them get lucky—there's a one-in-a-hundred chance that the founders will get lucky and bootstrap their way to success. Perhaps one in one hundred times the product happens to be really good and original. But if you look at the failures—the 99 out of 100 that fail—many also have original product ideas. With entertainment media it's hard to tell in advance what's a hit and what isn't. This is generally believed to be true about all entertainment media.

The bootstrap approach to starting a business has never appealed to me. I wouldn't want to start a company unless the idea was a big one and then I'd ensure that everything was first class—first-class money, first-class advisers, and a first-class management team. There's no reason to take a lot of risk in those areas. Creating a start-up in a first-class way dramatically improves your chances.

Okay. Let's talk about your big idea for Electronic Arts (EA). The idea was to treat computer game programmers like artists.

Actually, EA was about three big ideas. That was one of them. The business was more than simply treating programmers as artists—as creative people. It would be more accurate to say that we brought a methodology for managing a creative process to what had traditionally been an engineering methodology. This translated into a certain style of recruiting, managing, and rewarding creative people. It also translated into a production process methodology that more consistently, like a cookie cutter, cranked out good titles and products. In the music profession you can't buy a record and hear a single chord played out of tune. In the software business almost everything you buy has mediocre product value. What we did was to say, "Why not treat the talent like they're treated in other professional entertainment fields?" That was the first idea. The second idea was direct distribution. Until then nobody had ever done direct distribution—it was all done through distributors. Frankly, nobody who is anybody in entertainment doesn't do their own distribution. This way we could get shelf space for every product and therefore minimize our dependency on having a hit product.

So the trick was to leverage the retail channel by providing a broad assortment of products?

Yes. Our third big idea was technology leverage. At that time nobody had a planned approach to technology development. We were the first to invest in building a system—almost like a studio. Try to imagine what life in the music business would be like if you had no recording equipment, no professional studio gear, no synthesizers, no nothing. We built what we called the artist's workstation, which was the system we used for creating products for multiple formats. Doing so made us efficient in dealing with the lack of standardization.

So, EA was really a combination of three things— a creative process methodology, direct distribution, and technology leverage. If you think about that combination as a strategy you'll realize that you must apply more capital and commit to achieving a certain market share. Otherwise the whole model fails. It's like getting a 747 off the ground; with enough thrust and enough lift you can fly. Once off the ground the plane is passenger-mile efficient. Most of our competitors hadn't incorporated any of our three aspects of strategy—much less two or three of them. Had we done only one part of our three-pronged strategy we might have failed from simply being out of balance.

It is an interesting approach. Did you understand all these points of leverage at the outset? You already had 135 competitors and were relatively late in the game.

We clearly laid it out in our business plan. What I'm saying is that the key to risk reduction is to figure out the right strategy. The right strategy for us was combining those three elements and determining the amount of money we needed to implement that strategy. We raised more money than our competitors raised. Most of our competitors were bootstrapped companies. Brøderbund was one of the few that raised any venture capital—a couple of million dollars by 1982—but they sat on the money. We were the first company to use capital as a strategy. What's interesting is that people frequently say that the way to manage risk is to spend less money, to take on fewer initiatives, to do less.

So, the fact that there were so many competitors demonstrated to you that there existed real opportunity for a well-funded company?

Yes. Now we're coming back to entrepreneurship. Here's a key thing to remember about being an entrepreneur: a true entrepreneur is a creative person. Creative people don't do things to make money. They do them because they have no alternative. They *have* to do it. They have to get it out. So, as an entrepreneur, you don't sit there looking at the number of competitors and think about whether you can beat them or not. You don't have an objective, rational process. You need a certain amount of confidence in your invention. To an extent you're insulated because there are many things that you don't know will go wrong. If you knew in advance of all the things that could go wrong, as a rational person you wouldn't go into business in the first place.

Did you do any market research before starting EA?

I did enough. I had the idea for Electronic Arts when I was in college. I worked at Apple as a means to an end. I knew I wasn't going to stay at Apple forever, but I knew that before I could start a software company there first needed to exist hardware to run it on. So I helped build the market for this equipment and learned from others about running a business. I'm surprised that I stayed at Apple as long as I did—four years. It was such a rocket ship ride. In 1975 I told myself that I would start my own company in 1982. When 1982 rolled around, I felt like I was a bit late because there were other companies, like Brøderbund, already out there. They weren't doing very much, but I was definitely behind. Fortunately, I was able to meet anybody in the industry I wanted to meet. I helped start another little game company called SSI with a young game fanatic. I went to game industry trade shows, like the West Coast Computer Fair. That's when I was able to test the hypothesis for Electronic Arts. It was clear to me that many creative people didn't have a clue about how to handle the business side of things—I knew I could offer that to them.

What things, in retrospect, would you have done differently?

A paradigm shift occurred in the industry. Atari was collapsing, this was pre-Nintendo. It was a very tough time because many people wrote off the game business due to Atari's collapse.

Atari was synonymous with games.

Yes. It's unusual for a consumer product company's economic struggles to be so well known. It poisoned the well for many consumers because games suddenly became unfashionable. It wiped out the industry for a couple of years. We should have started the company two years earlier when the tide was in. We built a boat and launched it just as the tide had gone out. It would have been easier if we had launched two years earlier or two years later, but that kind of thing is hard to anticipate.

Let's focus on this. The market is drying up, you've just launched a company and you're sitting there in your office. What do you do?

This is the difference between an entrepreneur and an operating executive: most entrepreneurs don't understand how to operate a business. There is a huge amount of common sense and courage involved in operating a business. You don't need too much more than those qualities.

Most entrepreneurs lack common sense. They may be courageous about their inventions but they're not courageous about things like layoffs because most entrepreneurs are optimists. What you're really looking for in a management team is the right balance between optimism and pessimism. You've got to conserve resources very carefully. Generally, the typical entrepreneur is optimistic to a fault and always has forecasts with hockey stick projections—"We're about to take off....hang in there another couple of months and we'll take off"—it's bullshit. No entrepreneur ever even comes close to the forecast. Once you've been through this a few times you know it, the venture capitalists know it, and pretty much everybody knows how to deal with it.

I'm very satisfied knowing that I'm a good operating executive because of what I did in a series of crisis situations. I'm not interested in being labeled as an entrepreneur in the classic sense. Most of these new companies either come out of the chute and fail or they start growing and the entrepreneur gets the ax because he doesn't manage the growth. Or the company may grow nicely for a while, but the entrepreneur doesn't know how to build the management team. Often when these young companies start to go fast it feels like a World War I biplane trying to go Mach II: the canvas peels off the wings.

Do you think having an M.B.A. gave you the necessary skills?

Probably the most valuable course I took as an M.B.A. was Interpersonal Dynamics. The second most valuable was finance, which explained net present value. I'm not sure there was anything else. I certainly learned technical details about cost accounting and how the accounting system works, but I could have learned that in college. In retrospect, had I not gone to Stanford, I could have gotten started in the industry two years sooner and wouldn't have been any worse off, because those were two pretty interesting years. As it was, I practically worked full time my second year in business school—I just couldn't wait. Everything was happening and I wanted to be there. I did market research and consulting projects pretty much from the spring quarter of my first year.

So the M.B.A. didn't help?

Like I said, entrepreneurship is about being creative. You must be able to think big. You must be able to see things differently and come up with big ideas—not just the product and company concepts, but creative ways of managing the business. If you're going to run a business successfully there are many general skills you need, but much of it comes down to common sense and courage. You've got to face reality.

If you took a hundred middle managers, you would find that the majority of them wouldn't be able to tell a subordinate he or she wasn't performing. Another thing very few managers can figure out is when a workforce reduction is needed. People are generally unable to deal with confrontation or bad news, but frankly, if you're not dealing with the bad news, you're going to fail. I don't mean to say that you should have a culture based around criticism, per se, but if you don't know what's going on, you won't learn very much. These are not things that you must, or can, be taught in school.

Business schools are incredibly arrogant. At Stanford I took a course in sales force management that tried to teach me how to manage a sales force of 400 people, but I could not take a course in how to sell. I had to go to an outside school, like the American Management Association, to get a course in selling. The same applies to public speaking. There are basic skills that are fundamental to doing almost anything in life that a place like Stanford Business School won't teach you.

Then what are business schools' value?

They'll teach you esoteric things. I would never hire a Stanford or Harvard M.B.A. from a consulting firm like McKinsey or Bain & Company. It's just total bullshit. It's absolute, total bullshit. They can't help me. Maybe they can help a Fortune 500 company that is completely clueless about its business. But you can't tell me that some kid fresh out of school is going to teach me something about my business that I haven't observed myself. If that's the case, boy, I've really screwed up. If that's the kind of help I really need, how screwed up must I be?

Some say it's the hand-holding and reassurance they provide management.

Right. Sometimes it's just politics. Sometimes big companies have to line up outside credentialed resources to justify what they want to do.

You mentioned the need for courage to survive a difficult business climate. Can you give us an example of a serious threat that almost put EA under?

It happened continuously. The first seven years were like that.

And how did you handle it?

For example, we had three layoffs on three different occasions in that seven-year period. A couple of times we reorganized and shut down a couple of companies we started. Managing these crises is the most important skill I, as a business person, have. It's probably the most important one for many people. You've got to be resourceful. Common sense and courage, combined with creativity, is resourcefulness. It's the ability to recognize what is really happening. The first step is: collect the data. You'd better have your finger on the pulse. The second step is: analyze and figure out what's wrong and why it's wrong. Then you'd better have the courage to fix it, and fix it now. Some companies fail because they don't study what's going on, and don't have a reasonable picture of what's happening. Others have a reasonable picture of what's happening but don't want to believe it— they're in disbelief. At others, people may understand what's happening, but are afraid to deal with it.

To me, that is what resourcefulness is all about—collecting information, analyzing it, figuring out what's wrong, and coming up with creative ways to fix problems right away—and pulling the trigger. It's incredibly scary and incredibly stressful. It's not much fun having a layoff. It's not much fun shutting down a business that you started. We shut down our first business in Japan after a year. It was almost like Dunkirk. It was something like, "Whoa man, we don't have a clue here. Let's get the hell off this island. Let's get out of here. Pull up stakes! Get out! Get out! And let's not come back until we figure things out."

If your executives are not doing the job, you must be able to pull the trigger. We brought in someone to be our lead marketing guy. I thought he was great. He thought he was great. He had great credentials, yet we had to fire him three months later. Again, you must have the ability to figure out what is really going on.

So, given EA's poor start, how did you turn it around?

Like I said, the tide had gone out. We hit our forecast the first month. The second month we were off. The third month we were off by more. The fourth month we had a layoff. We cut back spending, hunkered down, and tried to conserve cash. That improved things quite a bit. We looked at the executives who weren't really cutting it and got rid of them. We regrouped. We fired sales reps who didn't produce. CEOs in companies like this one will spend a certain amount of time running every department. You probably can't afford a full team at any one time anyway. So, at any given point in time, the CEO is running more than one department anyway.

You can't afford a full team?

That's the way I look at it because you can't afford to spend the money. I would say that EA is pretty typical; I usually did three jobs aside from what I was supposed to do. When you're small and growing, that's the way it is. Later, when the company gets big and there is an asset to protect, you can afford to keep the CEO in a purely strategic role figuring out how to grow and defend the asset. In the beginning, you're just paddling as fast as you can. There is a benefit to doing the job yourself because you learn how things get done. It makes it much easier to hire people for those jobs because you really understand the different requirements and it's easier to manage them. One of the more valuable aspects to a startup situation is that you've had your hands in every part of the business. I'm not talking about being autocratic or looking over people's shoulders. It's a matter of not being disconnected and out of touch.

At EA, we had issues in sales and marketing. We had to figure out how to generate more revenue. That's another phase you go through as a small company: learning to be really creative with revenue generation. You can come up with literally dozens of ideas for making money.

You've been able to create alliances with many large companies. Is being a dealmaker a talent of yours?

I don't think of myself as a dealmaker. I consider that more a means to an end.

You've given equity stakes to Matsushita and AT&T in your new venture, 3DO. Has this hurt you in terms of preserving autonomy?

No. Company control doesn't, in the end, have that much to do with ownership. Certainly, if you are a subsidiary and one company owns a controlling interest, then they'll feel like they own you and will cast a pretty long shadow. But if nobody has that kind of position, then the question is whether or not these corporate partners can gang up to disagree with management. This situation applies to any CEO at any company. If you're off your rocker they can get rid of you. That's the main thing the board is supposed to do. If you're doing a good job and you're managing an effective process, the board will support you. It's not really an issue.

So in 3DO's case it's not that big an issue?

That's right. Ironically, with the 3DO board, even though most of the board members have a corporate agenda, they've helped more in developing a company strategy than the EA board did.

The EA board was just a bunch of independent board members. It was more difficult to get them to support what the company needed to do. Perhaps it was harder for that particular group of people to understand the business and accept what needed to be done. A classic example: It took me a while to convince the EA board that we needed to move to the Sega platform. Again, conventional wisdom would say, "That sounds very risky, they're going to sue you." Where would EA be today if we hadn't moved to Sega? It would be a pretty small, insignificant company. To be honest, it wasn't that pleasant for me having to convince a lot of people what needed to be done.

If you feel very strongly about a strategy, you must figure out a way to convince people to support it. It's one of the things you don't realize until you've done it for a while. If you're any good as a CEO, part of your job is to be smarter and figure things out before everybody else. And if you can't, what the hell good are you? Why the hell should you be the CEO if you can't do that? This means that if I figure out a problem and a strategy for dealing with the problem, I've probably figured it out before other people have.

So you had to convince your EA board of directors that a layoff was necessary?

If you go to the board and tell them that you want a layoff, they'll be very supportive. Conventional wisdom says that management usually spends money and hires people. It implies that things must be serious if the CEO comes to the board saying that he's screwed up, should cut spending, and reduce headcount. All the board will say is, "You're not severing any major organs, are you? As long as it's only an arm or a leg or a hand." Pretty procedural things will happen at that point.

That brings up the question of why you were the best CEO for EA.

EA is an unusual combination because obviously, there's a big creative component to the business. I'm creative and I understand how to manage creative people and the creative process. I also got into the business because I really liked the product. Having a personal feel for the product helps a lot. Third, I'm a pretty good businessperson. Any business requires it, but when you look at the computer industry through the 1980's, you'll see that many companies were successes. Many times the success was driven by market growth. For example, when I was at Apple, we all thought we were the cause of the success, but we weren't. We were just lucky to be at the right place at the right time. The whole industry just took off. That's the only time in my life I've had the opportunity to be in that kind of situation. It's only later on, when you realize that things don't always work that way, that you feel lucky. Many companies experience that kind of a growth and suddenly articles appear about what geniuses the managers are. Then the first thing goes wrong, the wheels come off, and they are suddenly losing money. Many times such market growth will hide real mediocrity in the management or in the strategy.

In games, it was really a tough business throughout the 1980's. There was no slack for anybody. The fatality rate was very high. In fact, out of the 135 companies at the start, only ten of them were still around five or six years later. There was incredible turnover of companies.

Tell us about the headaches you face as the manager of an established company. Is it difficult working with large corporate partners like AT&T?

Yes. AT&T has turned out to be our worst nightmare as a corporate partner. People usually think, "Big companies—solid, reliable." Well, they change direction more often and are completely ruthless about dropping things. In fact, EA and Matsushita were the real key investors in 3DO in the beginning. We assumed that by giving them equity, we would cement them as partners, but equity didn't really do it. The reason it didn't is that most companies are really driven by their operating P&L statement, so partners like EA really concentrate on quarterly revenues, profits, and license terms.

What about your VCs?

EA is a classically funded startup—we had three major venture firms who were involved and contributed well. My experience with venture capital money is that I only work with absolutely first-rate venture guys and only want first-rate thinkers if they are going to be on the board at all. Nonetheless, I didn't let them take over the company when they wanted to. We had a lot of problems in 1987. We had to deal with product transition issues and too much expansion. So we had a layoff, shut down some businesses, got refocused, and developed new growth strategies. The board and the venture guys, by Spring of 1988, were getting really, really nervous.

The funny thing was that EA was already half way through the solution at the time they were panicking. We had already done half of what we needed to fix things, but the results weren't going to show for six months. That was the only time when people on the board thought that they should cut my head off and try somebody else. Some people in that situation probably would have allowed it to happen but I didn't think that was the right thing for the company, so I hung in there tougher than others would have. At that time the VCs would liked to have changed the board in order be in a position where they could pull the trigger on me. I made sure they couldn't do that. Some of it was politics but some of it was ensuring I did the right thing and maintained the relationship the best way I could. The downside to venture guys is that they sometimes think they know more than they do about what's best for your company. They're accustomed to a certain level of performance in companies and in company management. Many times when they want to take over and make executive changes, it's probably the right thing to do. But they don't want to admit it when they make mistakes. If they fire the CEO and the guy they bring in screws things up, VCs say: The other guy was a disaster anyway. Well, maybe he wouldn't have been. Who knows? I'm not here to defend anybody else but I know that the VCs were definitely wrong to think that getting rid of me was the solution, and based on what happened since, they would certainly agree with that assessment now.

When I started 3DO, I just didn't want to go through that ordeal again. I wanted [venture capital firm] Kleiner Perkins in the deal for two reasons. First, [venture capitalist] Vinod Khosla is probably harder working, by a factor of ten, than any other venture capitalist. There is so much more value having him involved because he's a talented operating thinker, a strategic thinker, a good negotiator, and he'll spend time helping you. Other guys just won't do that. A lot of venture guys are just bankers: show up for board meetings and that's it. Vinod had a good feeling for what we were trying to do; he had a strong personal interest in it. Second, I didn't want 3DO to be in a situation where everybody on the board had some vested corporate interest and therefore didn't necessarily care if the company made money. Venture capitalists, on the other hand, only make money if the company makes it. It's a nice influence to have. Although the corporate influences have never really been a problem with 3DO I think that's mainly because of the high level of class of the individuals involved.

What's the key to success in your business?

It's leverage. It's pure and simple.

What you must realize about capitalists is that capitalism is no longer like Economics 101. It's no longer about building a better product. It's no longer about being more efficient and offering a better product than your competition. Business is now a big Monopoly game. When you talk to venture capital guys about what they're trying to do, they're not trying to make a successful company or product anymore. They're trying to look for situations where they can have commanding market share and really drive it using, frankly, techniques that are supposed to be illegal, but the government doesn't seem to care about anymore. Everyone looks at it that way. In a business such as this one, companies are saying, "How do we achieve critical mass and control things that give me the leverage to squeeze more profit out of that critical mass?" Don't misunderstand me: I'm not willfully disobeying the law. That's not how I look at it. That's the way all these VCs look at it. They want Park Place and Boardwalk with a bunch of hotels on them.

If that is the case, what advice would you give to entrepreneurs who lack the access to huge sums of capital?

There are a couple of different ways to approach this issue. The first thing to note is that someone who's a real entrepreneur doesn't need anybody to tell them to start a company. They'll just do it. I once asked one of my venture capitalists, Don Valentine, if he was politically active in trying to get special tax treatment for capital gains and he said, "No, it wouldn't make any difference in my business." I said,

"Gee, why is that?" He said, "First of all, my limited partners' money is municipal, tax-free, fun money. Second, the difference in capital gains profit wouldn't affect the behavior of entrepreneurs at all." And he's absolutely right. Absolutely right.

So, a real entrepreneur is just going to do it. Nobody can talk them out of it. A real entrepreneur needs to get a good lawyer and become objective about having a good plan and a good team—ensuring the team has the skills to succeed. On the other hand, you can't tell most entrepreneurs anything. They're pretty opinionated about how to go about things. They must learn from their own mistakes, and the ones who do learn from their mistakes and adapt will be the successful ones.

There is a second approach for people who have a desire to start their own company, but don't have a specific product idea or vision. I think that's a lot more difficult. Perhaps it's possible for someone with the right training and the right business discipline. I remember a venture-funded company that was started around the same time as EA—Spinnaker. It was started by two Harvard Business School grads who had been working for Boston Consulting Group. Their approach was to look for a business to start by doing a study to determine which industry to start a company in. Right from the beginning I thought, forget it, they're history. They never figured out how to make any money. The company is still around in some form but they're long gone. The company just never really got anywhere. They were able to raise enough money from people who believed in that approach to starting a business.

On a personal note, what lessons have you learned about balancing your personal life with the demands of starting a company?

I've learned that it's very tough to manage a family life and a business. Many people try and don't succeed. I was married once before to a woman partially because she wanted to start her own company. The situation provided some intellectual attraction but it didn't necessarily make for a stable, long-term relationship. We never saw each other.

Today it's tough to balance, but when things are busy my wife and I make the time by scheduling dates in advance and sticking to them. My advice is to either find someone who's willing to support you and your career or to go it alone.

13

ED McCRACKEN

Silicon Graphics

MEDITATIVE MANAGEMENT

Ed McCracken is the chairman and CEO of Silicon Graphics, Inc. (SGI), a company that designs and manufactures visual computing products. Though best known for providing the technology that created stunning visual scenes in movies such as *Jurassic Park* and *Forrest Gump*, the majority of SGI's products are sold to companies in nonentertainment industries such as the automotive, aerospace, pharmaceutical, and petroleum industries.

SGI was founded in 1982 by Jim Clark, a Stanford electrical engineering professor, along with six other graduate students. Clark designed a microprocessor which allowed computers to display three-dimensional graphics very rapidly and enabled scientists to create visual models of complex natural phenomena. Although the market at the time was small, the company grew rapidly and revolutionized automobile design, motion picture special effects, and molecular DNA modeling. Ed McCracken joined the company as president & CEO in 1984 after a 16-year stint at HP. Clark left in 1994 to start Netscape, the internet software company known for its popular product, Navigator.

McCracken grew up on an Iowa farm. His father, a corn farmer by profession, attended William Penn College, but ran out of money and returned home. McCracken remembers that money was so scarce his family lived on what could be considered a subsistence farm—the family couldn't buy anything it didn't raise. McCracken saved for college by raising 4-H prize cattle from the age of ten.

His formal schooling began in a one-room rural schoolhouse. A high school teacher named Illiff Leu encouraged McCracken's interest in electronics, which he studied at Iowa State University (he donated several million dollars to the university in 1992). He received his Stanford M.B.A. in 1968 and went on to become group general manager in HP's computer systems group until his departure for SGI in 1984.

Soft-spoken, calm, and low-key, McCracken does not fit the stereotype of an intensely extroverted and wrathful CEO; in the tumultuous environment of the computer industry, McCracken relies on meditation to improve his intuitive sense and to spur his creativity.

This creativity has certainly helped SGI's revenues. In ten years at the helm, McCracken saw revenues go from $5.3 million to more than $1.5 billion. Today Silicon Graphics employs more than 5,000 workers worldwide. Despite its stock performance, the company has been sued by shareholders several times—lawsuits which McCracken characterizes as "extortion and blackmail" and has testified before Congress to encourage protective legislation.

"Serious fun," as the company defines it, is considered a vital part of SGI's atmosphere. Ping-pong tables and soft drink vending machines are found throughout the company headquarters while conference rooms are christened after movies in which SGI technology was used. The company sponsors bungee-jumping events and lip-sync competitions, and has even held wakes for divisions that have been merged into others.

As a corollary to the philosophy of working closely with the customer, McCracken feels that long-term product planning is dangerous. "We don't do long-term planning," McCracken is known to say. "In fact, we try to stomp it out." McCracken feels that this allows the company to incorporate new features into its products, and quickly adapt to and accept the rapidly changing and unpredictable environment in the industry.

In the rapidly changing visual computing industry, the future remains unclear. Many believe that interactive programming—either video-on-demand or the downloading of television shows whenever desired—will constitute a significant portion of the multimedia industry. The question remains, however, whether the device consumers will use to watch this cyber-programming will be a PC or TV. SGI has placed its bets on interactive TV trials in Orlando, Florida—one of the first in the nation.

Heavily involved in civic activities, McCracken was named co-chair of the National Information Infrastructure Advisory (NIIA) council in 1993 by President Clinton. The NIIA advises the government on the information superhighway and addresses controversial issues such as electronic commerce and privacy rights—significant public policy topics given the highly diverse information now available on the internet, ranging from bomb-construction to hate groups.

If, however, the information superhighway is to remain accessible to all Americans in the future, McCracken feels that proper education of America's children regarding the information superhighway is necessary. "Students receive little or no direction about the proper conduct in today's computing culture," he concludes. In response, the NIIA launched NetDay in 1996, an initiative to wire hundreds of elementary and high schools to the internet.

We interviewed Ed McCracken at SGI's worldwide headquarters in Mountain View, California.

"CEOs have this obsession to know everything and control everything—that is stupid."

You were extremely successful at HP before you came to SGI. What made you leave?

I think some of it was personal. I really enjoyed running a division at HP. I was very effective at it. And then, because it was so very successful, we broke it up into multiple divisions and I became part of that "in-between layer" in HP, between top corporate management and the division employees.

And I found that I didn't enjoy that job and I wasn't extremely effective at it. I really wanted something that was a little bit more hands-on, externally focused, rather than internally focused. I really liked the customer environment. I liked the technology, and I didn't like all the other stuff very much.

So, when SGI came about, I had a chance to come over here and meet some of the people, and saw the value-added in the company. It didn't take long to get a whole new track going, and I was over here.

You didn't really enjoy your growth and your progress in administration at HP?

When I joined HP I assumed that I was going to stay there for a maximum of five years. And then it turned out that, every year, things were getting so much better for me at HP, it was hard to leave. And I was enjoying it. As long as things were moving so quickly for me at HP, it was hard to leave.

We've heard a lot about HP's culture from the other CEOs that we've spoken with. Do you think you brought some of that culture over to SGI?

Some of it. I learned a lot at HP. It's a great place to learn. I learned a lot about core values. Some people think our culture here is somewhat like HP, because it's derived from it. But, it's also quite different, in that there's a little more intensity about being on the leading edge, that wasn't as prevalent at HP.

Why do you think that is? Why do you think SGI is more intense, compared to HP?

Well, I think it's maybe because of the time in which we grew up. Hewlett and Packard, both wonderful people, came out of the World War II generation, that had a different set of values—perhaps including a little bit more institutional responsibility for the individual.

Whereas we grew up in a time where information-age individuals wanted to take responsibility for themselves; they didn't want the company feeling responsible for them too much. And there's so much more industry here in Silicon Valley, so that if you don't succeed here, you can go down the street and try again. It isn't that you're going to work for Silicon Graphics your whole life, probably. But the idea of the HP core values is, you're probably going to work there your whole life, and, this is not part of the new world.

Plus, the computer business is changing rapidly; it's a chaotic world, the time frames have condensed dramatically. You need to be able to make decisions quickly, and get on with them and get the job done. And that's important. It's also important you don't miss a generation, or else you're dead.

So, as the stakes have gone up, the time frames have gone down. At HP, I always felt that I could really work hard and make anybody successful who worked for me. Here we don't have time. If somebody's not cutting their own way, then you just don't have time to deal with it, as their manager. So, it's much more of an intense culture here. Unfortunately, in the computer industry, there's no place to hide.

Looking back, do you think you'd do anything differently regarding your transition from HP to SGI?

I really can't with my philosophy. I almost never go back and try to rewind history. And, it [SGI] is a real success story. And if I had it to do over again, I think I'd be lucky to do the same thing. So, I don't know.

When I came on board, it was a real disaster here. We had great people, great technology. The people here had done a project, and it was a good research project. But, the product didn't work, and we had a hundred people. And the worst thing about it was that there were only two or three people in the company that knew the company was in crisis. They had kept it from everybody else, because they thought it would impact morale negatively.

Of course, the first thing I did was to call a company meeting, explain the whole cash situation, what our options were in terms of big layoff, or somehow saving enough money and designing our second generation in time to really solve the problems.

And then the rest is history, and that is we designed the second generation in six months without laying people off, for $500,000 a month, and we went out and raised another $10 million just in case, which we actually didn't use before our IPO.

And, we all lived. But now a lot of people appreciated it [calling the company meeting], and we have developed this culture of sharing information and no secrets and disclosing everything and having everybody be part of the solution.

And you think that sharing information is one of the things that defines SGI's culture.

Well, it's, it's one of them. I think the whole idea of an information-age company is to get as much connection as you can up to the nodes of the organization, so that as the nodes make decisions, they're going to make them within an overall context. Because you want them making decisions as much as possible. Because it's quicker and better.

How do you ensure that the information that you transmitted to the nodes is accurate? That is, when you send a message down five or six layers with 80 percent of the message accurately being transmitted, then there is an accuracy level problem.

Well, you don't try to communicate through different levels; you communicate directly. You find every opportunity through the Web or through electronic mail, or through any means to go directly. I'm doing that with the company right now.

I mean, the old idea of the fifties organization, where, you worked as a manager with your staff, and then your staff worked for their staff, and their staff worked for their staff—it doesn't work that way here.

Everybody here is trying to learn—analyzing the black box, trying to understand how it works, and its advantages and disadvantages. And in the end—everybody shares the same kind of data.

In terms of learning, you were quoted as saying that the military indus-try was driving a lot of your technology, but now it is Hollywood that's doing it—

Yeah—Hollywood certainly is an important part of our future, and I think we've attracted Hollywood for two reasons; one is we enjoy it, and all of our employees enjoy it, and the second is that Hollywood is full of people who are not satisfied with today's technology.

One of the criticisms we've dealt with since the beginning of the company is all these people out there who say, "Having that great technology is so expensive, but who needs it? You can do whatever you want with a PC."

And, people have been saying that now for twelve years. People in Hollywood know better. They know you don't do these kinds of things with PCs. Our market tends to be characterized by people who know that you can't do these things with PCs. Technology drivers.

We've tried to define your driving characteristics and came up with: unassuming, analytical, and humble—(All laughed.)—in a pretty big way. I went to a speech that you gave recently, and there were about seven or eight times where you just said, "I don't know." And I thought that was such a departure from most of the—

—from Scott? [McNealy of Sun Microsystems]

(They laughed again.) *Well, without naming names. I decided it was pretty unusual—*

—You know, CEOs? CEOs have this obsession to know everything and control everything. I mean, that's stupid. You can't know everything. You can't control everything. In the information-age organization, you want people in the nodes to know everything associated with what they're doing.

We have a learning organization. So, if you feel like you know all the answers, you can't learn, and you probably don't belong at SGI. Understanding those new paradigms before other people do is our corporate strategy. We have to be able to learn. You have to be the best technologist working with the best customers in a learning mode.

And the result of that learning is understanding new paradigms, and then implementing that existing technology, putting that right into a silicon, if appropriate, and getting that into the marketplace five years before the commodity players. That's what gives you the fifty percent gross margin and lets you spend ten to twelve percent on R&D and twenty percent on selling, and have a model of innovation.

So what are some of these new paradigms?

It can go all the way from specific things like morphing and texture mapping and graphics, to the importance of the Web, to parallel processing with software that's programmable by mere mortals. It's ample range, but, our company has consistently introduced the kinds of technology, the kinds of systems that are at least five years from the commodity players.

When you have to constantly introduce these new technologies and at the same time keep growing as a company, how do you find the right people? You recently hired a lot of people, and in the process stated that you didn't want a "bozo invasion." How did you manage to do that?

When you hire lots of people you do make some mistakes. But, generally, I think, we have done an excellent job. The issue we ended up having was that it took a lot of time. So, we didn't really plan as much for having our managers so heavily involved in recruiting that they had less time to do everything else that they had been doing. So we found that there's a tremendous delta [change] between growing at 30 to 35 percent, and growing 40 to 50 percent. That delta is seemingly pretty innocent, but it really isn't because we have all the natural feedback in our company that grows 30 percent. But if you try to go 40, 50 percent, you've got to really work at it, and you can only really work at a handful of things, as a manager. We've had a few issues like that that we've kind of worked our way out of now. We've gone through the pits of hiring all these people and trying to integrate them, and taking all the time to do that.

We've slowed down now. We're tuning up the machine, and you can feel the machine getting more aggressive and more tuned now than it was six months ago.

You've had phenomenal growth over the last few years. How much of SGI's success do you think is just luck? Some of the CEOs that we've spoken with feel that it's all luck. Do you believe that?

Well, I certainly agree with, whatever you call it—karma or whatever else—there's a lot of that in everything. I grew up on a farm in Iowa, and I really appreciate the farming mentality because you work really hard—and then you let the weather happen. And some years are good and some years are bad. You don't have much responsibility for it. It's what you do, rather than the result, which is important.

But, I think our company also gets a lot of really great people. I've never seen the kind of talent we have in any other company. So, you combine that with the fact that we've had ideas that are truly revolutionary, that just really changed the industry.

With every person we hired, it seemed like we had new options. We hired the multiprocessing team almost by accident. During a period of time when the computer industry was collapsing, including Silicon Valley, every year some company would fail or be close to failing, and we would be able to reach in and grab the top five percent of the people and bring them into Silicon Graphics, with a set of technologies associated with the new people.

That's probably the luckiest thing that happened to us, actually. It hasn't been true in the last two years; we've had to get back to college and recruit people, because the industry is so strong right now. We actually were better off as a company when the industry was less strong—now everybody does well. Everybody does well, and so everybody's growing and everybody's being successful.

It gets a little worrisome when it's survival of the fittest, and it becomes increasingly difficult to have opportunities to actually not only hire great people, but also gain more market-share points. It's really hard to gain market-share points right now. We're doing it, but it's harder because everybody else is growing 15 to 20 percent a year, and we're growing 30 percent a year. It was a lot nicer when they were growing zero and we were 30 percent.

What about your different management style? There is a lot about you in the press about being meditative, introverted, and this is in contrast to most of the CEOs that we've met with. Why do you think you've been successful with this leadership style?

To me, the important thing about being a CEO—about being a manager at any level—is to learn who it is that you are and bring that into the job. It isn't that there's one model of a successful manager; there are a lot of models. I hope the book really deals with that. And the important thing is to understand who it is that you are and amplify that, and bring that into the job, and be comfortable with it.

So, I bring who it is I am, and Scott [McNealy] brings who it is he is, and Andy [Grove] brings who it is he is, and they probably all work, and that's fine. My wife taught this course at the business school on leadership styles with Michael Ray [a professor at the Stanford business school], and they talked about the enneagram— the nine different leadership styles, etc. And I think it's really pretty good stuff. What it really teaches you is that you have to develop your own leadership style.

It's different from when I went to business school, when they had a class teaching that there was one leadership style. We listened to the equivalent of Jack Welch. Everybody would try to be like Jack—well, that's stupid. We're not all like Jack Welch.

Do you think that certain leadership styles are suited for entrepreneurs, and does Ed McCracken have that type of style?

You know, I doubt it. I think I'm really good when I take an idea—working with a true entrepreneur, like the Jim Clarks of the world, the valley is full of them—that's beginning to gel with a small team, and then I can really work with that and turn it into something that gets pretty big, and leverage it along the way. I've done that over and over; I've done that at HP, I've done that here. I really enjoy doing that. But, am I someone who can go off and team up with some people in a garage somewhere and start a company? Probably not. Probably not me.

Why not?

Well, I'd probably find it boring.

Boring?!

I just wouldn't get much stimulation out of it. I find it boring.

We've talked about the skills and assets that you bring to SGI. How do you think you fail SGI? What skills do you lack and how do you compensate for that?

Well, I mean, you've mentioned some of them. I'm quiet, I'm introverted, and I like to play with ideas. And I've figured out in my mind the right direction to go, I lose a lot of interest in it. So I try to surround myself with people that are much more interested in execution, implementation, getting the job done, schedules, all those kinds of things, because, in the end, I'm not as well cut out for that.

And again, I think that managers need to know themselves and not try to do everything themselves. They need to surround themselves with people that will complement them, rather than duplicate them.

We're going to ask you some tough questions now—

—I thought you had been.

*I remember hearing you on NPR one day talking about shareholder
lawsuits. You basically said that a lot of shareholder lawsuits are really
unjustified, that they cost so much for the company, in terms of time
and effort, that companies are forced to settle. But, how do you explain
the plaintiff's premise that you guys really are—*

—Crooks.

*Right. And you're not letting shareholders know the whole story, and
that they have every right to know because you're working for them.*

I mean, I can't imagine that every CEO in Silicon Valley is a crook. I
think almost every company in Silicon Valley has been sued multiple
times—companies like Hewlett-Packard and Intel and ourselves. And
when somebody is sued, and when there is a big settlement, the people who get the money aren't the individual shareholders. They're
really Bill Lerach [a prominent plaintiff's attorney] and his friends,
who have made so much money out of this, it's unbelievable. So
they've had quite a business going for themselves.

*There are rumors that their business has dropped down considerably
after the recent legislation limiting shareholder lawsuits.*

Well, it has dropped down somewhat. I'd just like to take a very visi-
ble stand on this. Four years ago, I really got upset with the whole
thing. We settled our first case for a few hundred thousand dollars.
But that's the last one we settled. From then on, we decided to take
everything to the mat. I testified in front of the Senate on it; I've
been very active on this issue. The House and Senate passed it, and
Clinton vetoed it—which I was disappointed in—but they overrode
his veto.

Why do you think Clinton vetoed it?

Well, you'd have to ask him. But the plaintiff's bar is really active in
Democratic politics. I've never met a Democrat in Washington, D.C.
who hasn't received major funding from the plaintiff's bar.

So, I think it was practical politics. He didn't fight the veto override very much; in fact, he made, near as I could tell, zero phone

calls on that. So it was easy to override the veto. There may have been a deal involved, for all I know.

But, it's a big deal. I've tried to convince every company CEO I know not to settle anymore of these and encourage them to take it to the mat. We've done that, and as a result, it's not quite so easy pickings any more for them.

Eighty percent of investors are pension funds and institutional investors. *They* don't like these things either; they know better. They're not going to get a return on their investment by these lawsuits, and generally, our long-term investors make a lot of money on our stock and have done so historically. So, I just don't have much tolerance for this.

Do you think these lawsuits affect your business relationships with customers?

No, it doesn't affect the business, but it certainly has affected our relationship with Lerach. In fact, he just sued us again recently, even after the legislation. And so, we've given them a target, certainly, and we knew that would happen, and the fact is that that has happened.

One of the things you've stated is that you really don't do much long-term planning at SGI. Compared to many other companies, this could be considered in sharp contrast.

I think some people around here would do more long-term thinking than a lot of people do. I mean, you think about the market in the year 2000 or 2005; we try to understand the new paradigms. We try to project all these ideas; try to understand how things are going to be.

You just don't lock it in. So, we try to limit the things we need to make a long-term, hard decision on. We tend to focus our long-term thinking on core competencies and the general direction of technology in the marketplace, whereas we focus our tactical thinking on as short a term as we possibly can, and try to keep every decision open to the last possible minute. And then when we make the decision, we implement quickly.

In terms of long-term thinking, SGI has been very active in promoting interactive television, and there appears to be almost a dividing line now between PCs and set-top boxes. Where do you think SGI's future is headed? Do you think we're going to have PCs? Or set-top boxes?

Well, I think we're going to have both.

My personal belief is that, if I look at the data for the home PC market, as I understand it, about a third of the homes have a PC, and that hasn't increased a lot in the last year. I think the PC market has run into a brick wall in terms of the home marketplace. Getting PC usage to 50 percent of the population is almost impossible. So a third of the homes are going to have multiple PCs, or Macs or whatever.

But I think that the *rest* of the population, the two-thirds of the population, is not going to use PCs unless it becomes an appliance: an appliance where the PC-ness is masked, and that becomes television or whatever else. And so, by far the bigger market is the non-PC home market, which is currently being fulfilled only by video games and video game machines. But it will be eventually fulfilled by interactive television and Web—you'll turn your television into a Web terminal. That's a much bigger market.

So my belief, with the technology getting faster and faster, is that any market is going to change by a factor of a thousand, in terms of price/performance between now and the year 2010. It's not going to get locked-in in terms of the exact paradigm. In other words, the PC monopoly is going to gradually get broken in the next ten or twenty years. If you ask me how it's going to get broken, I don't know. But it's going to get broken, because you just can't carry that kind of paradigm in the future for that period of time. Things are too chaotic. Consumer electronics will be one of the things that breaks it.

So you think it's going to be PCs or interactive television? I mean, are people going to be able to do their word processing on a TV?

Who would want to use their TV to do word processing? So—what I'm saying is that two-thirds of the population doesn't do word processing.

Even in the future?

Yeah, for the next 10 or 20 years. It's hard for us to imagine that, but yes, two-thirds of the population doesn't do word processing. They want to sit down with a beer and watch television. More power to them. It's great. Or they just want to sit around and play video games. Super.

That's why I've been leading this U.S. Advisory Council in NII [the National Information Infrastructure]. The Clinton administration has been very supportive of using new technologies in K-12 education. I think that could change all of this. We can educate a whole group of K through 12 students, who will move in this society, will have a different set of characteristics, who will kickstart the country into the information age.

Can we talk a little about Net Day? With such a chaotic marketplace and all of your potential competitors, it's amazing that you've been so involved in it. Why are you so involved?

Well, I think part of it is to change this two-thirds of the population. I think it's the only way to have a country without the haves and have nots. It isn't so much an economic question; it's who's exposed to this—

—Knowledge and education.

Right. I think that Stanford has talked about "TAF-letes," children of technically advantaged families, and the advantage they have in the 21st century. Well, the only way to get everybody in our country an equal start, which is what we believe in—we don't believe in equality in our country; we believe in an equal start—and the only way to give people an equal start is to introduce aggressively this kind of technology in our schools, so that everybody has a chance to really explore what the network means and what the computer means. I hope this becomes a standard part of the education process.

But, it's expensive. The U.S. Advisory Council talked about it taking three percent of the educational budget in order to introduce this kind of technology in the next five years. Three percent is a lot of money. The cost is broken into the four compartments: the networking expense, the computer expense, the teacher training expense, and the content expense.

And Net Day takes care of a large percentage of one of those: the networking expense. It really does wire our schools. We still have the other three-and-a-half components. Those are still expensive. So, Net Day has a lot of criticism from those who say, "That's not the answer. They're just wiring our schools."

And, of course, it isn't the answer, but if it can save a half a percent on the educational budget as a result of doing it, what a wonderful thing. And if it can bring communities together, work together to improve their schools, also what a wonderful thing.

So, I think it's great. And our company is involved primarily with disadvantaged schools in Silicon Valley, where we're doing the wiring. We've really offered to do that, rather than being in the situation where we would just wire schools—that were going to get wired anyway—a little more quickly. So we're trying to wire schools that wouldn't have gotten wired for the next five or ten years.

What about the content part of it? Having schools wired to the internet provides kids with access to some wonderful things, but it also exposes them to things that perhaps they shouldn't be exposed to. Do you think there should be censorship of certain materials on the internet?

I don't know the answer to that. I think the heavy-handed things that are being talked about aren't very appropriate and are probably not constitutional. On the other hand, I think that the part of the internet community that feels that there should be no regulation of any kind on the internet has got their head in the sand, too, because society has a responsibility of some kind for the internet—the same kind of responsibility we have with newspapers and radio and other types of public communication.

The problem is that we have a new paradigm, a new way of communicating, and a whole set of legislators who have never used the internet. And their job is to cut new legislation that relates to this new community. So, I think those of us in the internet community are worried about this, because we've got a group of people who don't have a clue, but are passing the legislation that regulates those of us that *are* on the internet.

On the other hand, I think if we had a team of educated legislators, I think it would still pass some legislation that related to certain types of rules about—rules of the road. There are also filters of various kinds that allow the internet to be used in schools, without as much risk of pornography and the kinds of things that people are worried about. So, my belief is that censorship of the internet is not something we have to do in order to use this technology in our schools.

If you were a young person looking to start a company, what area would—

Content. I think it's going to be big for the next twenty or thirty years. That's where a lot of the venture capital money is going, whether it be content for the Web, or content for anything. It's a wonderful opportunity. My venture capital friends are telling me that many of the ideas they're seeing for new businesses are coming from people under 26 years old, and they all relate to some kind of content, rather than some kind of Web tool. But I think content in general is really hot—there's going to be a dearth of content compared to the appetite out there.

You've talked about the need for balancing your family life with your work. How do you manage to do that, and what kind of advice would you recommend for both of us trying to start companies?

You know, I don't have the answer to that. I think the important thing is to really be happy, and if you're really happy, I think that your family life's going to be better than if you're unhappy. And your work life's going to be better than if you're unhappy.

So, it is a tricky thing. There aren't obvious answers. I'm not sure I have the answers. But you have to work at it. In the end, the people doing these kinds of jobs don't separate family and work very much; I'm doing this job because I love this stuff.

And if I really separate it totally from my family, then I have to live two different lives, and I have to balance them. If there's someway I can integrate it and have it be one life, then it works better. And some of that you can do, some of it you can't do. Integrate it into your travel schedule, integrate it into your life. But I don't have all the answers, I'm still learning about balance.

But what I've also learned is that I'm not happy if I choose not to be absolutely involved in the current technology revolution. Because I get a lot of excitement out of being an active participant in today's computer environment. And as a result, I can bring more to my family situation.

So, you feel that your being involved in technology *helps your* family *life?*

It makes me much happier. I could give it all up, but I would be a less happy person. I might be able to spend more time with my family, but it wouldn't have as much quality.

14

KEN OLSEN

Digital Equipment Corporation

REFLECTIONS ON THE REVOLUTION

Fortune magazine hailed him as America's most successful entrepreneur. His unauthorized biographers call him "The Ultimate Entrepreneur." His company experienced 25–40 percent growth for seventeen straight *years*. At its peak, Digital Equipment Corporation—known as DEC by outsiders—employed 120,000 and claimed annual revenues in excess of $14 billion. For 35 years Ken Olsen, founder, president, and *pater familias* piloted his company from a modest start in a small Massachusetts town in 1957 to a formidable, if bloated, leviathan at the time of his departure in 1992.

For all the attention that CEOs of companies one-fourth Digital's size manage to attract, Olsen should be as familiar to America as any of the great industrialists this nation has seen. However, a certain modesty and aversion of publicity make it difficult for all but his closest colleagues to know him.

Olsen received his M.S. in electrical engineering from

MIT in 1952. After working in MIT's Lincoln Laboratory on a joint development project with IBM, Olsen saw that an opportunity existed to create a computer radically different from the closed architecture Big Blue locked its customers into. In 1957 he and colleague Harlan Anderson approached Georges Doriot, the godfather of the venture capital industry, for $70,000 to start a company.

Digital's first computer was the PDP-1. Though it fueled the company enough to achieve critical mass, subsequent computers like the PDP 4 and 6 failed. It was a backbreaking effort to deliver the PDP 8, but Digital successfully ushered in the state-of-the-art in interactive computing—the notion that users needed to access a computer using their own terminal and keyboard in order to perform their work, rather than submitting requests to lab-coated managers in imposing data processing centers packed with IBM equipment.

By the mid-seventies, over 70 competitors crowded the minicomputer market that DEC had spawned. The firm's technology lead had steadily withered and IBM had awakened to the minicomputer market opportunity and developed a system of its own. Even Data General, the company founded by the departed Digital lieutenant, Ed De Castro, had racked up some successes. Once again though, Digital reestablished dominance with a next generation computer, VAX. VAX carried the company for another decade and fulfilled prophesies of computer ubiquity—for companies, at least.

For most entrepreneurs, the calls to step aside and let professional management guide the startup venture come relatively early. Olsen survived these challenges even during the company crises of the mid-70s and 80s and propelled his company to greater heights. By 1992, however, DEC's financial outlook was bleak; the company had made several aborted attempts to enter the PC market. Olsen's disdain for this emergent industry was well documented by the press. More than once, when asked about the next wave in computers, Olsen responded with "There is no reason for any individuals to have a computer in their home." This assessment of the new market for years was held up as emblematic of corporate arrogance and ineptitude.

Nonetheless, Olsen's legacy of achievement marks him as a truly successful, if somewhat contrarian, entrepreneur of the modern computer industry—a giant to be reckoned with.

A company of firsts, DEC implemented various unorthodox business practices, including paying its sales people on the basis of a strict salary instead of leveraged incentive plans popularized by IBM. At the height of the company's success, DEC's unique approach to business was hailed as revolutionarily effective. As the company plunged, pundits and employees complained about overlapping tasks, committee-managed inefficiency, and chaos.

From a cultural perspective, DEC mirrored Olsen's temperament—unique and unpredictable. Digital was the countercultural antidote to IBM—a title Apple would inherit in the 80s—yet it was decidedly un-flashy and almost entirely avoided TV and radio advertising. In short, most important aspects of the DEC gestalt inevitably trace back to Olsen himself.

We met with this publicity-shy bear of a man at the offices of his newest venture, Advanced Modular Solutions, in bucolic Boxborough, Massachusetts.

"The best assumption to have is that any commonly held belief is wrong."

You are one of the most successful entrepreneurs of your era. What are some of your keys to success?

I was asked to give several speeches on entrepreneurship to various groups this Fall. One point I made is that business schools' goal today is to teach people to become entrepreneurs. I think this is a serious mistake because once someone becomes accustomed to being his own boss, it's very hard, maybe impossible, for him to later work as a team member. People who want to be boss right from b-school are skipping the beneficial activities of working for somebody else—not very likely the best thing to do.

My recommendation is to first work for somebody else and learn how to be a team member, which sounds kind of obvious, but in this modern world being a team member is very odd. Then go and learn to be a leader. If you never learn to be a leader don't try to run a business. Television business schools don't train people to lead. They teach that the boss must be decisive, even if he knows nothing.

Someone who teaches at West Point and Harvard compared the two educational systems in an article. He wrote that one is always questioning issues and never cooperates—Harvard. The other is disciplined and military. He didn't come to the obvious conclusion that Harvard's way is better. You really need both. Whether it's Harvard, or MIT, or Stanford. You're kind of useless in business with just an academic background. You're also useless if you spend too much time in the military. You really ought to have backgrounds in both. There is a lot to learn in the military about leadership that the academic world completely misses. The image of the military may be of top-down management, but that's not how it works.

I was a sailor. A ship is a good model for a business. A captain determines the direction of the ship, but the ship is made up of many divisions and groups. Each one is quite independent and knows what its particular task is. And the attitude is beautiful, shared, and universal. The attitude is that the ship may not accomplish its mission, and the group may get killed, but one thing is for sure: it isn't going to be our group's fault. People don't sit there worrying about the captain and the direction of the ship.

So it's a deep sense of accountability that maintains high performance?

It's more than accountability. The group members simply know how to do their task well even if nobody else on the ship knows what that particular task is. Business needs such a model, too. The manager who says, "I make all the decisions"—is a fool. He's a fool.

Can we take that model further? How do you instill such a sense of mission in sailors or employees?

I'll tell you a little story about Digital that illustrates this.

Digital Equipment started with $70,000. The nice thing about 70,000 dollars is that you can watch each one of them. We had a twenty-person committee and I was chairman, the only one with the P&L statement in mind since everybody else was full of ideas for spending money—wonderful ideas like printing matchbook covers for marketing—really intelligent things. I kept saying no. They got very frustrated with me, went to the board of directors and said, "Ken is a dictator," which was true, because if we had enacted all the proposals to spend money, there wouldn't have been anything left.

Our other problem was that the employees weren't very smart. They couldn't understand anything. By the time we were a $14 million company we got into trouble. I went to Boston to speak with General Doriot [of the venture capital firm American Research] and told him something had to be done because we didn't have things under control. I thought that we could sell ourselves to Singer. He wasn't terribly sympathetic nor was the board terribly sympathetic because we were very profitable and growing fast. Then the profits deteriorated. I announced that we were a new company as of that day—we were now following [former CEO of General Motors] Al Sloan's model. Sloan broke his company into business units and said that management's job was to leave them alone. I declared that we were, as of then, organized into five business units. It went over like a lead balloon. Several people quit—no exaggeration. One very competent fellow said, "I'm 33 years old. I'm *not* going to take orders from a 30 year old." Not one person in the company liked it. They went home and told their wives that they had been demoted, which is impossible because mathematically not everyone could be demoted. The board of directors was dead set against it. One director, the one who introduced me to Al Sloan, said he would sue the company for fraud. General Doriot said, "Ken, I'll support you. Anything you do. But remember, no one ever succeeded at doing this."

I religiously followed Sloan. To this day I don't think Digital's board of directors understood the model. They'd say, "Ken's a little funny. Real managers make all the decisions."

The loneliness of my position cannot be exaggerated. But miracles happen. If you look at Digital's growth and profitability after that decision there's a distinct discontinuity: our growth accelerated—an absolute miracle. All of a sudden I was no longer the terrible dictator because I was now in a position to criticize the managers. Those same people who had been so dumb became geniuses. The people who before were frustratingly dumb, made the basis of Digital's success. Do you see the secret there? The genius on my part—I have to tell you this because you wouldn't notice it—was to follow Al Sloan religiously: Leave People Alone. I'm sure that when General Doriot said past attempts at such a business model never worked, it was because top management couldn't leave people alone.

Nobody at the top is smart enough to know everything. Nobody is so competent they can do everything for everybody. The problem is that very few people realize they can't do everything and can't make all the decisions. Very few board members understand this because to them, the ideal manager dresses well, speaks well and makes decisive decisions. They love that. You see it on television all the time.

So your management secret was really just borrowed from Sloan?

Jack Welch of GE says he got the idea from one of my speeches. I'm not sure that's true. Hewlett-Packard is doing quite well following this model now. Some say they got the idea from me. Of course I say no. It was Al Sloan.

It's interesting that during this organizational change—a critical juncture in Digital's history—your employees thought the company was a failure.

No. They weren't even conscious enough of the sum of it all.

But weren't they unhappy with the state of affairs?

They weren't that unhappy. They had a lot of freedom and had nothing to compare themselves to. It was just clear to me that we were in trouble. The strength of the new system was in making the P&L statement near and dear to the people making decisions.

The only word I can use to describe the budgeting process is "travail." We made money hand over fist because managers had power and responsibility for a budget and plan that worked. This is what made Digital. The one weakness was that the employees did very well and after a while the success went to their heads. That's when the whole system fell apart. The system depended on the struggle and the travail. General Doriot used to say, "When you say your prayers at night, pray for inventory."

Pray for inventory in what sense?

Just inventory, because it's a big deal if you have too much or too little. I said, "When you say your prayers at night, pray for your P&L statement." That's a secret of success. When you're making too much money, you get careless. That's when the business falls apart.

When do you think this took hold at Digital?

In the late seventies.

And prior to the seventies?

Prior to that, in general, things went very well. Our way of business worked because business unit managers had very close contact with their sales people—it was clear to the business unit managers how things were sold.

Something else emerged from running the company this way. Because of the pressure for economy, employees built a common set of products. Most companies have different products in different parts of the world even though they don't have different business units. Since our employees were all interested in economy there was a common set of products. This meant a lot of meetings and a lot of discussion. Critics thought that all the time Digital employees spent talking was a terrible waste. While talking was sometimes frustrating, the result was a common set of products.

When I tell people, "Say your prayers at night, pray for your P&L statement," I also say, "If you pray for your spreadsheet, it won't answer you." Spreadsheets just devastate people.

The introduction of spreadsheets was considered a great new tool for business management. Why are they harmful?

Because people started believing them. All the numbers in business are garbage.

Why is that?

People believe that the computer must be right. At Digital I never looked at the financial statements.

Let's get back to the comment you made about success getting to peoples' heads and destroying the company.

Athletes, actors, politicians, even preachers. They can't survive success.

How can you avoid the trap?

I failed at it, failed badly at it. I believe, however, that the solution lies in the accounting system. If we had the discipline of thoroughly maintaining our accounting, we would have known how well or how poorly we were doing. Even the board of directors got careless because there was so much profit. In the late 70s and early 80s the success had gone to peoples' heads and I couldn't straighten it out. We had no new products for five years. The company spent five years introducing controls and red tape to protect us from making defective products, and nothing came out. I'd ask, "Why don't you make a new product?" The response was, "It takes two years to get it all worked out. Why start today?" With no new products eventually things collapsed. The profits disappeared.

An interesting thing happened. All the vice-presidents quit. They say I fired them, but they quit. And the *Boston Globe* proclaimed that it was The End of Digital. Interestingly, not one of those vice-presidents succeeded on his own. They did very well at Digital because of the supportive environment.

Several of them did try to start their own companies.

A number of them did. They thought themselves the greatest managers on the earth. They thought that their presence at Digital made the company a success—and that their presence at their new companies would make them successes. Management at Digital had this attitude that the company was successful just because they were there. And I wasn't able to control that attitude.

The message is that part of doing things the business unit way is to not look for credit for yourself. When I was a little kid I learned the fable of a turtle who talked two ducks into holding a stick between their mouths while he held it in the middle—off they flew. One bird said, "This is clever, I wonder who thought of it?" The turtle couldn't resist saying, "It was mine" and down he went. Part of the secret is to avoid showing the world how smart you are.

So your secret is to downplay your successes?

It's more than that. You've got to make sure that people take responsibility for their jobs. The accounting system helps them take that responsibility.

How did Digital's culture reinforce the sense of responsibility?

I can't describe it. I'll just talk about it. It was very much a team spirit, a family spirit, an overwhelmingly strong one. As far as I'm concerned it's very important that a company have a trusting spirit of teamwork—love is almost the word. For example, a hurricane once hit our Puerto Rico facility. A whole bunch of Digital people helped. We flew a DC-3 down there every day and people here sent baskets of apples.

Once somebody at Digital got seriously ill and died three months later of cancer. People wouldn't even ask—they would just take time off from work and visit him in the hospital. That's a family feeling. You just know it's the right thing to do.

Then when everybody [including Olsen] was fired, what fascinated *The New York Times* was that former Digital employees stayed in touch with each other. Today there are alumni groups all over the world.

How do you instill that sense of community?

I don't know, but it was all over the world. In Japan there were two thousand people. It was almost like a religious revival. They were that much of a family.

It's interesting. When we trusted people in the organization, we rarely had dishonesty. We had complete trust. It was a beautiful feeling that you took for granted—you just trusted everybody. That doesn't mean we didn't have some really miserable people at times.

How do you deal with the miserable people?

I never did figure that out either.

Balancing work and family pressures always seems to be a big issue for entrepreneurs. You've worked in the industry for over thirty years. How do you balance your home life with your work life?

You definitely have to work at it. One bit of advice I give people is, if you're going to learn to be a manager, take responsibility in your church or town activities. This actually relates to the story of how I got into business. I was an engineer at MIT and had all the things I ever wanted to do. I went to an old church in Boston, and in those days it seemed that only old people went there—I was thirty years old in a church full of old people. They asked me to run the Sunday school. Immediately I went to Dixon library and checked out all of the books on business management. It was my first exposure to the academic approach to management. That is what introduced me to business. What I did in Sunday school to make it a success, and what I did as a sailor, and what I did at MIT was to make the environment interesting for people.

How did you make business interesting?

Before MIT I spent a year at IBM. I designed the circuits for a computer we made but I never told anybody I did it. Just introducing them made everybody very excited. At Digital I would often do things without telling anybody and got people jazzed up. I didn't need the credit and it made things exciting. That aspect of leadership really helps a business. People who are successful usually have ways of exciting people.

Getting back to the question of balancing private life, how did you manage to spend enough time with your family?

I just made it a point to. I backed-off from a number of different activities. I was on a number of company boards and I backed-off on those. I've always made it a point to be with the family. I'd often get my work done by getting up early before anybody else. I still get up before anybody else. I hate to be cheated from that time. The secret is to do the work when it's quiet and you're alone, sometimes at three in the morning. That way no one thinks you're cheating on family time.

Could we talk about another interesting aspect of Digital—your decision to use noncommissioned sales people?

You could say that what is commonly believed is almost always wrong. No one on the board of directors ever understood the idea behind noncommissioned sales people. They didn't understand anything.

It all depends on how you think of a salesperson. If you think he's a professional and you want him to act like a professional, you treat him like a professional: "Your job is to sell. Your satisfaction comes from doing your professional job." The problem was that management couldn't leave the noncommissioned plan alone and snuck in a commission plan. It took a very thick manual to explain the plan. In effect, the message to the salesman was, "Memorize the manual and focus more on knowing the rules than on the products you're selling." You can see the harm in that. Management just couldn't leave their cotton-picking hands off the sales plan. Like the income tax system, it got more and more complicated.

People always approached me and said, "I've got a product that doesn't sell. Let's temporarily have a commission plan for it." I said no. "You'll always make dogs for products. By putting a commission on the dogs you end up selling the dogs and not the products customers really want."

Everything gets messed up by paying commissions on the dogs. The same thing is true with piecework. I have a friend who was a wood-cutter. He made a lot of money. I called him and said, "I'm giving a speech on commission plans and piecework. Piecework pay must really work in the woods because you simply get paid for the amount of wood you cut." He exploded. He told me that after getting paid for piecework, loggers at one company were running in the woods and driving machines faster in order to get paid more. Finally the logging company paying piece rates had to fire the whole crew because the accident rate was so high the company couldn't pay for the insurance.

People have this naïve, stupid idea that everybody is motivated by money—it's common knowledge. When I left Digital the company of course went whole-hog into commissions. They never figured it out. The sales manual, I understand, was real thick. It's too complicated.

The common belief about commission plans is, "Boy, what a chance we have to manipulate people!" Trying to manipulate people is the wrong attitude. The results are just terrible.

So when you created a noncommissioned plan, your objective was to motivate people by...

—Just saying, "You're a professional and we expect you to act like a professional."

And the means for instilling this motivation?

No, no, no. You're talking like a manipulator again.

But you did want people to be proud of their professional work.

Yes.

What do you think motivates employees?

There are always a certain number of people who are motivated by power, jealousy, and vindictiveness. In my last years at Digital I didn't do a good job of getting rid of that influence. Most people really want to be proud of their work. And if you encourage pride in one's work you will end up with people who are proud of their work. When you go to work every day it's terribly important to get the satisfaction that you're doing something useful or successful. In general, people are more satisfied if they're expected to be honest than if they're expected to be dishonest—you end up with a different class of people. Most people want to work for positive reasons, not for some arbitrary commission plan.

Could you talk about your later years at Digital and the difficulties you experienced?

I have to be careful because I don't want to publicly criticize the people there. Remember that our primary goal at Digital wasn't to have the fastest computer. We never had the fastest computer—almost never—because our commitment to customers was that future computers would run the same software the previous one did. This gave us an enormous customer following. But it also meant we couldn't use the latest fads.

The goal was to protect customers' investments.

Right. We also built a large service organization. Our training group was bigger than most universities—it was huge. If you think of that training group as a marketing tool can you imagine customers spending a week paying university-level prices to be lectured about your products for a week or two? You couldn't beat that as marketing. Customers swarmed in. To the stock market and the board of directors this just looked like a wasted effort on Digital's part. The analysts and the board said that the goal should be to have the fewest people per dollar of sales. Apple was probably the best in the industry on that basis. Apple did no manufacturing, no selling, no servicing, and had no customer contact.

We did an enormous amount of consulting at good rates; it was very profitable—there was no inventory or other costs. Customers loved it. And the sales people were there to be helpful to the customer. At almost every large customer account, we had an office right in the heart of the company and had access to everybody because we were a key part of their organization. We had an office at Ford Motor

Company—we owned Ford Motor Company. The same was true of Bell Labs because they trusted us. To those with business school backgrounds, our business model was too complicated. A good business model was defined as selling a product, getting rid of it, and just focusing on making the next product. The whole industry was run that way. So you can see why the board of directors said, "Digital has 110,000 people for only a $14 billion business. Get rid of the people, about half of them."

That's what they told you to do?

Yes. Cut the workforce in half—outsource, get rid of them all. This fit in with the stockholder value that Wall Street wanted.

Let's switch gears and talk about your longevity as a CEO. What motivates you to continue working and to even start another company after such a long tenure at Digital?

It's a little complicated. The satisfaction comes not from others seeing or understanding one's work. It's in yourself. It's the satisfaction of seeing the results, even though no one else knows of your achievement.

It's commonly said that Ken Olsen lost it, that he didn't know the mainframe was dead and that the PC would take over the mainframe. They still say that even though the world has now determined the mainframe will be here forever.

I'd like to answer the accusations, which are foolish. Aside from that, the big motivation is seeing something accomplished. I still spend a lot of time designing equipment. I can do things that almost nobody else can do. I have some background in toolmaking, a little in physics, a little in chemistry, and other things. I enjoy putting that all together. I can stay up all night working on it.

Why does that motivate you?

As you get older and you pass the normal retirement age, can you think of anything better than having an exciting job? Sitting down and watching television or playing golf rates much lower on the list of accomplishments.

You mentioned that the press said you had stayed too long as Digital's CEO. When should a manager or an entrepreneur leave his or her company or job?

That depends on a lot of things—when he gets tired, when the job is no fun, or when he really has lost it. I was on a mission then to show the world how business computing could be done. People within Digital were just too embarrassed to have an old man doing that. The greatest dishonesty was that they destroyed VAX. So few people understand the significance of business computing. Mainframe computing runs reliably every day—no one watches it. It is by far the least expensive form of computing. PCs are the most expensive.

The stupidity of computer science is such that if you go to any computer science school and ask, "What's the answer to the problem with computing today?" They say, "The answer is to have faster networks, faster PCs, and big databases where you can mine all that information—and then make graphs."

It sounds beautiful. Many companies today are in trouble because of that kind of thinking. It was these kinds of ideas which five or six years ago tagged me as being too old for the business. Everybody knew that PCs were going to take over the world yet it's clearer than ever that the last thing you want is a PC running anything important. Five or six years ago PCs were much better than they are today.

Like other successful companies, Digital had defectors who left to start their own companies. One of the best known was Ed De Castro and his company, Data General. How do you minimize such defections?

I'm friends with De Castro now. It's been a long time—you don't hold hurts. This sort of thing will always happen. The miracle was that we decided not to sue them, to not make an issue out of it, and very rarely comment on them in public. In retrospect this was marvelous wisdom. Suing them would have dragged on for years. It destroys your heart. Jealousy does terrible things to people—the yellow-eyed monster that eats one's heart out. Vindictiveness and the pursuit of revenge, just because someone wronged you, is destructive. The wisdom was in not pursuing the issue and controlling the urge for vindication.

That takes incredible restraint.

And it's logical. Jealousy and vindictiveness are not the best inclinations to have because the task is to win business by doing a better job than anybody else. This is what you should spend your energy on.

Some people thought, "If that's Ken's attitude, let's take advantage of him." So once in a while we did nail somebody in court. It was usually people who sued for trivial things like a real estate activity and figured that Ken could be taken advantage of. But we didn't do that in the situation you mentioned. It would have dragged on forever.

So what you're saying is you can't keep people from taking company knowledge to start their own companies.

No, you can't. You must know that it's a part of business. Certain things can't be helped, and you live with them. You get mad for a while but it's not a very useful emotion.

Ed came to see me not long ago. There is no point in even remembering the incident anymore. He has a jet airplane and invited me to go flying with him. It's so much better that way. It's so much better not to hate people. Those who do often end up suffering quite a bit.

You've had a long career. Any regrets?

Oh yes. As you can guess, I think a lot about what I should have done at Digital during my last ten years there. It's been fun, satisfying, and exciting, but I'm usually more conscious of my weaknesses and mistakes than I am of my successes. In many ways that's healthy—if you're blind to your weaknesses you get in trouble. I don't think about any of the successes at Digital. I look forward to doing something new each day.

You only learn if you're conscious of the need to learn. If you conclude you're great, that's the end.

Did that sense ever take hold in you? Is that a regret?

No. I have a scientific and Christian background. The tradition of science is that you should think clearly enough such that you don't think you're great. Also, despite how things are presented today, traditional Christian background says that you really have no reason for pride. St. Paul said almost sarcastically, "What have you got that you weren't given? And if so, why are you so proud?"

Whatever you think you're good at is just at the surface of it all. There's nothing you're so good at that you really understand completely. When you get your degree in computer science or your degree in business they tell you, "Now you know it all. You don't ever need to open another book." I'm sure they do this because I've seen the results of people whose attitude is that they know it all. That attitude is so contrary to science and traditional Christian views it is obviously unwise.

Some people don't understand this: designing a financial system, designing an organization, designing a circuit or a computer diagram are almost the same thing—they generate the same satisfaction. The satisfaction is the same but there is much reason to be humble because there's so much one doesn't yet know.

Success in business is so fragile—human beings are involved, and the market is involved. People who follow somebody else's wisdom without thinking about it will miss these things. Being critical and analyzing issues ahead of time is satisfying. You must have humility if you're trying to figure things out differently from everybody else. But most people don't think at all. They fall in love with phrases. The best assumption to have is that any commonly held belief is wrong.

15

BILL HEWLETT

Hewlett-Packard

PEOPLE ARE EVERYTHING

Bill Hewlett and David Packard really are the patriarchs of Silicon Valley. Not only did they create a company which now employs over 100,000 people worldwide and is considered the father of the industry, they created a company with values—a company that treated its employees right, and had genuine concern for their welfare. They created a company with a management style that served as *the* model for the rest of Silicon Valley, and consequently, the rest of the world. Even at age 84, however, Hewlett is far too humble to accept such accolade without remonstration. And perhaps that—and not sheer wealth—is the mark of a true legend.

Hewlett was born in Ann Arbor, Michigan in 1913, but grew up most of his life in San Francisco. Hewlett's father, a physician, taught at Stanford Medical School. When he was just twelve, his father died of a brain tumor. Hewlett often reminisces that if his father hadn't died, he might have chosen a career in medicine. But, instead, Hewlett chose to become an engineer.

Bill Hewlett met David Packard in the Fall of 1930 as a

freshman at Stanford University. With the steady encouragement and guidance of Professor Fred Terman, Hewlett, Packard, and two of their friends—Ed Porter and Barney Oliver—were able to start a small company from their home. On August 23, 1937, Hewlett and Packard had their first official business meeting to develop "tentative organization plans and a tentative work program for a proposed business venture." In 1939, they formed a partnership and flipped a coin to determine the name order for their newly hatched venture. Hewlett won the toss.

After some time, Hewlett and Packard found a two-story house in Palo Alto that they decided to rent. The house had a one-car garage, which Hewlett and Packard decided to use as their workshop. The garage is now a California Historical Landmark known as the "Birthplace of Silicon Valley."

According to contemporary business school strategy, Hewlett and Packard's initial business approach was fairly unstrategic: they contracted out jobs, manufacturing custom devices such as a foul line signal for a bowling alley and a motor controller for a local observatory.

But, they soon realized that an invention of Hewlett's, the audio oscillator, held promise as a potentially viable commercial product, with applications in medicine, defense, and geophysics. Hewlett's audio oscillator was HP's first major product, and it became a big hit. The company grew like wildfire. In 1957, HP went public, and its commitment to innovation allowed HP to diversify its product line substantially. Nowadays, the HP behemoth makes thousands of different products.

Yet, during all of this growth, Hewlett and Packard maintained a commitment to their employees. They developed a code of values, called "the HP Way" which emphasizes a commitment to innovation and customer focus while at the same time fostering well-being in its employees and the community at large. The HP Way serves as a model for many companies today, both within Silicon Valley and throughout the world.

It is indeed difficult to overestimate Hewlett-Packard's contribution to Silicon Valley's emergence as the world leader in entrepreneurial activity, job creation, and technology inno-vation. And a large part of HP's success can be attributed to Bill Hewlett. With his humility, generosity, and sincere con-cerns for the welfare of employees, Bill Hewlett is truly a leg-end, and a role model for generations of future managers.

We interviewed Mr. Hewlett at his home in Portola Valley, California.

"You usually remember your successes and not your failures."

One of the most logical places to start is your association with Fred Terman, your professor. What was your incentive to take his advice and start a company and take a leap?

We were all in the same radio engineering class in college. The class was divided into two groups, one was the ham radio operators, and the other was the non-ham radio operators. Dave and I were in the ham radio group, and a very close friend of mine, Ed Porter, was also in this same group. Dave soon started taking graduate courses in this area.

Realize that this was in 1939, and that was no time to be starting a company. But it was almost as if we didn't have anything else to do—I think that it was probably the supreme optimism of youth. We were well trained, and we knew we wanted jobs, but we didn't know what they were.

A lot of people say that you need a completely original idea in order to start a business. Do you think that this is true? How did you get your ideas to make particular products?

We certainly didn't have an original idea. Our original idea was to take what we could get in terms of an order. Most of our initial jobs were contract jobs—ranging from just about anything. We did a ran-dom number of projects. I had worked on an audio oscillator. So, we wrote to a number of people around the country for orders, and sur-prisingly enough, we got some. And that's how we started in the elec-tronics business. It was an opportunity provided for us by a course in electrical engineering.

It was Dave's job to market it, and my job to produce it. So, he was the entrepreneur and I did the work.

Once you started the business on Addison Way, did you worry about competition when you became your own company?

There wasn't really much competition when we were doing the contract jobs. There wasn't much until we got into the oscilloscope and the oscillator business. There was a company in Boston called General Radio. The head of General Radio was a very cooperative guy. He said to us, "General Radio needs competition." He gave us encouragement and suggestions, which is unusual for a competitor.

One of the things that often gets overlooked in the history of HP, because it was such a success, were any mistakes that you made. If you were advising someone who was starting their own company as to pitfalls they should avoid, what would you tell them?

Well, I'll tell you that you usually remember your successes and not your failures.

Hmm. I don't know. It wasn't a clear channel from the garage to the computer—it was a big jump. And yet that was a mechanical jump—we did it step by step. We did it because our customers wanted us to do it. First, they wanted instruments, and then they wanted computers, and we did what they wanted. So it is really important to find out what your customers want, and do what they want.

You went away for a while and served in the war. How did that affect your role in the company?

When I left we had fifteen people, and when I came back, we had 250.

So, Mr. Packard was doing something right.

Yes. But, most of these people had second jobs. So, after the war, we cut down to 80 people. And that was a tough decision.

How do you handle that?

I guess the only thing you can really do is think of the alternative. If you don't let some people go, then the company will go bankrupt, and you won't be able to support anybody. It also helps to choose the best people and only choose those that you really need. The other thing you do is to really learn how to get the most out of your people—and that doesn't mean squeezing them, but rather creating a place for them where they like to work.

Let's talk about HP's culture. Everybody in the Valley admires the culture at HP and part of that stems from the HP Way. How did you decide to choose the objectives you chose? Was it a long, drawn-out process?

We had a management team, and we went to Sonoma one winter, and sat down over a weekend and talked about the company. At that time, we wrote down the corporate objectives, and really analyzed them. But, most of it is really common sense. The customer comes first. Without profits, the company will fail. A lot of these things are really just common sense written down.

We interviewed Ken Oshman, one of the founders of ROLM, and he attributed ROLM's culture to you and the HP Way. The whole idea of workforce diversity and progressive policies towards employees was pretty unusual in the mid-1950s.

Well, Dave and I did a lot of different things for the company at the time—keeping the books, making sure the product worked, developing new ideas. And, our friends were the ones that we worked with. They weren't employees, really. They were our friends. And so, it was important to us to understand how they felt about things in the company. It was important for us that all the employees were treated well and enjoyed themselves.

There was an instance where somebody became ill and had to take some time off, and needed money to pay his health bills. We discussed the situation, and we decided that the company should take care of it. But then, we thought to ourselves, "These types of things happen, and employees should be covered in these types of situations." So, we decided to offer health insurance for all our employees. [HP was one of the first companies to do so.]

So, ultimately we helped our employees. And, our employees helped us.

Let's talk about the centralization issue. In 1990, you and Mr. Packard felt that the company was becoming too centralized, so you went back in and instituted new training. How did you know that it was becoming too centralized?

The system was just overloaded. When you wanted to hire a new secretary, you had to go through five different levels. Overhead was killing us, and we couldn't afford to do this. At that time, Packard and I were retired, but we saw this happening. We said, "This is ridiculous! You can't get a decision made! Something is wrong with the system." So, we went back in and cut the decision time down and removed a lot of needless channels.

What was your guiding principle for selecting the right employees?

We didn't have business schools back then. And, we really had two types of employees: business employees and technical employees. We really tried to understand each other and complement each other. For example, Barney Oliver was an excellent scientist, and Noel Eldred was an excellent manager, so it was obvious where each person's expertise was.

You ran HP in the 1960s and 1970s. What do you think your strengths were as a manager?

Well, I learned from Dave, and Dave and I got along. I was really a technical guy in the beginning. And, Dave was a great manager.

"Getting along with Dave" is not an acceptable answer to us. (All laughed.) *What do you think your strengths are, really?*

Probably understanding people.

Do you realize that we grew up in the heart of the depression? And we hired people, not because they had the technology, but because they worked. And these people worked hard, and we wanted to share our profits with them. HP was one of the first companies that offered profit sharing to its employees.

We cared about our employees. We really did. It's not about the money. It's about showing them that you care. And that can mean giving them a blanket when a new child enters their home, or helping them when they are in dire need, or whatever.

For instance, we had these employee picnics with 7,000 people. And, Dave and I would help serve the food. And, there was one guy who always complained that the food was too well done.

So, we decided to serve him up some shoe leather. (*They laughed.*)

He came back and told us that that was the best food he'd ever had. (*More laughter.*)

How were you able to handle family life while working at HP?

Well, my first wife had a scientific background, so many of our conversations drifted over to science. I've got five wonderful children, and a dozen grandchildren. And, one day, my wife asked me, "Do you realize how much teaching goes on over dinner?"

But, even though I did work very hard, I tried to spend as much time with my family as possible.

Someone made the comment that entrepreneurs find it very difficult to work at HP because of the emphasis on a team environment. How do you feel about that?

That's true. It's unfortunate, but true. We've got some very good people in there, but they just do not fit the pattern.

Do you think that hurts the company at all?

Sure, but it also strengthens it tremendously. When a young guy comes in, he learns about the company a lot quicker because people are willing to spend time with him and help him, and that ultimately helps the company.

How important is integrity in the startup process?

Absolute. Without it, a company is sure to fail.

What kind of advice can you give people like us when starting a company?

Ultimately, you have to get each employee on the team. If they are on the team, your company has a chance of success. And, if they are not, then the company will fail. And the best way to get them on the team is by showing them that you care.

Let's talk about your philanthropy. Your foundation and you personally have given a substantial amount of money to various charities. How important is that for companies to do?

Well, when we became successful, we had a lot of money, but for years we acted as if we didn't have it. Our children all went to public high school and were raised like any other children. We tried to deemphasize wealth. But, we also looked at the problems that the world faces and felt that we could use the money to serve some purposes very well. Now, this was personal wealth. In regards to companies, if they can afford it, then they really should have philanthropic programs, because I think it adds to the community. But not if it is going to break them.

Finally, one of the comments that was made by one of our professors as we were writing this book was that it was all luck. Do you believe that?

Well, it's not all due to luck, but certainly a large percentage of success is. We were in the right place at the right time. We were lucky, and had wonderful teachers and mentors. HP didn't start in a vacuum. There was a lot of research in the area. And we learned from a tremendous number of people.

ABOUT THE AUTHORS

RAMA DEV JAGER is an MBA graduate of Stanford University Graduate School of Business, which is internationally renowned as a think tank for the high-tech world. Also a medical school graduate (Northwestern University), Jager has combined his medical and technological experience to form EMCard, a health care information technology company that provides hospitals and doctors with complete patient profiles loaded into a microchip on a disk the size of a credit card. He lives in San Francisco.

RAFAEL ORTIZ holds an MBA degree from Stanford University Graduate School of Business. Now an assistant professor at Stanford, he is also developing Apple Computer's new network architecture. Ortiz lives in San Francisco.